T0339825

# PLATO'S POLITICAL PHILOSOPHY

## The Cave

# Plato's Political Philosophy
## The Cave

## Roger Huard

Algora Publishing
New York

ISBN-13: 978-0-87586-530-0 (trade paper)
ISBN-13: 978-0-87586-531-7 (hard cover)
ISBN-13: 978-0-87586-532-4 (ebook)

Library of Congress Cataloging-in-Publication Data —

Huard, Roger L., 1954-
    Plato's political philosohpy: the cave / Roger L. Huard.
      p. cm.
    Includes bibliographical references and index.
    ISBN-13: 978-0-87586-531-7 (hard cover : alk. paper)
    ISBN-13: 978-0-87586-530-0 (trade paper : alk. paper)
    ISBN-13: 978-0-87586-532-4 (ebook)
    1. Plato.  2. Plato's cave (Allegory)    I. Title.
  B398.C34H83 2006
  320.092—dc22
                                  2006029710

Front Cover: Eric Fracassi's "Emergence"

Printed in the United States

To Shelley, my wife, my best friend, my muse.

## Acknowledgements

Unlike many works of this sort, I imagine, the present work was conceived and written within something of an intellectual vacuum. This no doubt will help explain many of its weaknesses as well as its strengths. There are however several individuals whom I would like to thank for their help, guidance and inspiration. They are, in order of appearance: Dr. Paul Savage, who first ignited the fires of interest in something greater than me, namely politics; Dr. James J. O'Rourke, who supported and mentored me in my first steps towards philosophic enlightenment; Dr. Dwight Waldo, who taught me that things that actually belong together don't necessarily look like they do; Dr. Jerome King, who gave me an audience and intellectual shelter when there were none; and finally Dr. William Connolly, who never afforded me the comfort of being his disciple.

Finally, I would like to thank my friend (and one time associate), Heidi Bloom, who was kind and diligent enough to edit, correct and suggest revisions in my manuscript where needed.

# TABLE OF CONTENTS

# CHAPTER 1. THE MYTH OF THE CAVE

Plato's myth of the Cave, which appears in Book VI of his *Republic*, is generally considered to be about the philosopher and his relationship to the political order he inhabits. It is also more specifically about the ancient Greek itinerant philosopher Socrates and his relationship to Athens, a relationship that, as most of us know, ended rather badly. Beyond this thumbnail understanding there are many interpretations of Plato's Cave myth that go into greater allegorical detail and mine its rich and varied veins of meaning. I will offer my gloss of the Cave myth but I will insist from the beginning that I make no claim about discovering Plato's "real meaning." Questions about what an author "really means" are inherently unanswerable and in the case of Plato's mythical story this is certainly the case. My purpose for reading and interpreting Plato is to understand more about the human condition as we experience it right now in the hope, ultimately, that I can share that greater understanding with others and that, in turn, this understanding may help some of us live a better, more meaningful life. This is a tall, even sanguine, order — I know. And it is all the more tall and sanguine because it not only aims to render our lives somehow better, but to do so by way of philosophic inquiry and understanding. But why else do it? And certainly, this would be a goal — in fact the only goal, I surmise — that Socrates and Plato would themselves credit.[1]

The Cave myth explores the philosopher's relationship to the political order by trying to explain how the appearance of things and the reality that stands behind these appearances work within the human condition. This ability to draw a distinction between how something appears versus the reality that in some way causes that appearance is quite possibly an aspect of the human condition that is unique to it. One simple example of this dynamic is the appearance of a rising and setting sun versus the reality of the earth orbiting the sun and rotating on its own axis. There is, I should add quickly, no easy or ready test for what marks an appearance as opposed to the real thing. Even the orbiting and rotating earth and sun are not the final word in this case on what is appearance and what is reality. Yes, the earth revolves around the sun; but as you move beyond the context of our solar system into the greater cosmic fold there is more to it than that. One finds that both the earth and the sun are "moving." We might even begin to suspect, as we investigate specific differences between what we consider appearances versus what we think is the reality behind them, that in fact all such differences are differences of appearance. It may be that we never ultimately get to the really real, that we never reach the thing-

---

1    I want to cut short as well any notion that what I am trying to do is exalt either ancient Athens as some kind of Golden Age or Plato as the pinnacle of moral and political thought. The mythical story I want to examine was written within a context that saw a *polis* put its most ardent patriot to death and finally succumb to the political rule of a neighboring conqueror — conditions that made trying to understand how one should live, individually and collectively, rather pressing. Perhaps we live in such a time; perhaps more so.

in-itself.[2] Humans are distinguished by an ability to see things in many ways, to make and interpret reality within many frameworks, to see a multiplicity of appearances whose validity depends entirely upon the context within which they are perceived. Humans after all have not stopped talking about the setting and rising sun, nor have we completely dispensed with the idea that the earth orbits the sun though strictly speaking that may not be exactly right or certainly is not the "real" or whole story.

I will not pretend or even attempt to resolve once and for all an issue as complex as the appearance-reality distinction. Indeed it may be more accurate to say that insofar as humans avail themselves of a distinction such as this, the notion that one could resolve it once and for all may be fundamentally wrongheaded. One thing is clear: we humans both understand and use the distinction between appearance and reality all the time. I would also add another observation that is certainly pertinent to Plato's Cave myth. The significance of the appearance-reality distinction rests with the existential ambiguities that define it and with the way we understand and handle those ambiguities both as individuals and as groups. In other words the key issue is not to determine definitively "what is appearance" and "what is reality" (perhaps ultimately a futile task), but to understand how human beings, both individually and collectively, draw and handle the distinctions they make (or fail to make) between things as they appear and things as they really are.

The reader may be puzzled by the tentative steps I am taking here towards a distinction that Plato himself seemed to acknowledge and promulgate so strongly. If any philosopher believed in and argued for the validity of the distinction between appearances and reality in a strong sense, then surely Plato did. Some might even go so far as to say that he invented or discovered the distinction.

---

2    There is for Plato unquestionably a "reality-in-itself" but I would argue that this is more an ontological thing (something that exists) rather than an epistemological event or achievement (something that can be known as such).

A summary of Plato's thought exists in the heads of many learned people and this summary frequently (if not always) sets unfortunate limits to what we can learn from his thought and, more generally, from the Classical Greek experience. Yes, Plato identifies and affirms the distinction between appearances and reality; however, this affirmation is neither simple nor straightforward. And, it is the myth of the Cave that can help us understand why this is so.

***

Before proceeding with my analysis of Plato's myth of the Cave, I want to take a moment to discuss what I will call throughout this and subsequent chapters the conventional and/or standard interpretation of Plato's political philosophy, especially as found in his *magnum opus, Republic*. There is of course no such standard or conventional view of Plato if by this we mean to identify particular individuals who hold this view or specific texts that articulate it. At the same time there are common thoughts and themes that usually accompany modern references or commentaries about Plato, especially when they center on his *Republic* and are of a summarizing or generalist nature. Indeed I suspect that many learned people who do not seriously study philosophy are likely to "know Plato" almost exclusively in these conventional or standard terms.[3] There are two elements of the "standard view" that I want to highlight. The first is Plato's idealism and the second is his authoritarian *cum* anti-political bent.

The idealism of Plato's political philosophy is primarily a function of the tight connection that he draws between this philosophy and his metaphysics. This connection is highlighted by the fact that at the top of both his metaphysical and political theories we find the idea of the good. This "idea," along with a host of other ideas that it underwrites and illuminates, is conventionally thought to

---

3    This is becoming truer as the curriculums in institutions of higher learning become more specialized and as a student's exposure to the "classics of western philosophy" becomes, at best, packed and distilled into one or two survey courses.

reside in a transcendent place that is (ostensibly) apart and different from the material world of everyday human existence.[4] I will
have reason to touch upon and even question this conventional understanding as our inquiry proceeds. At the same time I want to
make it clear that I will not engage in a full-blown epistemological analysis of Plato's idea of the good. My primary concern will be
to look at Plato's political philosophy through the lens of his Cave
myth — not to establish *what* the idea of the good is as such — and
to explore, among other things, how this idea works in his political
thinking and to indicate how our prevailing western notions tend
to misrepresent it.

Plato's authoritarian and anti-political tendencies, especially
as they are expressed in *Republic,* have been noted and commented
on by thinkers as ideologically diverse as Karl Popper and Sheldon
Wolin.[5] Even commentators who are less inclined to grind any axes
still invariably make note of Plato's despotic or authoritarian tendencies.[6] Of course the grounds for making this standard assessment
of Plato's political thought are in plain sight. Such notions as the
philosopher-king, the "metallic" classification of citizens, the strict

---

4    Few commentators doubt that there is a strong connection between
Plato's political philosophy and his metaphysics. The nature of this connection and more significantly the specifics about Plato's ruminations on
metaphysics are not so clear or readily agreed upon. The primary culprit
in this instance is Plato's theory of the forms, which gets its most comprehensive explication in his *Phaedo*, which is not a text that normally gets
bundled up with surveys or summaries of Plato's dialogues on ethical and
political matters. General commentaries about Plato's political ideas are
instead apt to use his theory of the forms, and specifically the idea of the
good as a backdrop to their discussion rather than its centerpiece. They
do not examine in detail what Gilbert Ryle called the ontology of Plato's
forms, see: Sabine & Thorson (1973) pp. 48-92; Wolin (1960) pp. 28-68;,
Wiser (1983) pp. 13-23; Brinton (1962) pp. 36-54; MacIntyre (1966) pp. 33-
56. In such surveys of Plato's political philosophy the theory of the forms
— especially and including "the good" — are assumed to be transcendent
ideas that exist in some other realm of being which is somehow connected
to the material world we live in. The particulars of this transcendent place
and its relationship to our world remains for the most part unexamined,
beyond the pale of political philosophy so to speak
5    Popper (1962) pp. 7-169; Wolin, ibid.
6    Cf — Sabine, ibid., Brinton, ibid., Wiser, ibid.

regulation of education and art, are all rather repressive sounding to the modern liberal-democratic ear. Even the most sympathetic of commentators are apt to excuse Plato's authoritarianism and claim that, albeit despotic, it is enlightened.[7] Plato's authoritarian measures in these sympathetic renderings are conducted in the interest (or for the good of) each citizen. Unfortunately, this is an explanation all tyrants and despots (not to mention parents) employ to justify what they do. It's not hard to see then how Popper would find in Plato the intellectual roots of totalitarianism or how Wolin might accuse Plato of curing a city's political problems by eliminating the activity of politics altogether. I will argue in what follows that most conventional or standard views concerning Plato's authoritarianism are significantly misleading, significant because they distort and sometimes efface some of Plato's more pertinent ideas or arguments about political reality. Again my focal point will be Plato's *Republic* as interpreted through his myth of the Cave.

***

## The Story

In a cave sits a community of people. Their heads and bodies are bound in such a way that they cannot see themselves or the people who sit with them. All they can see is the wall directly in front of them. Directly behind these seated "prisoners" is a freestanding wall. Directly behind that wall there is a road along which other "people" carry objects above their heads so that these objects are just above the height of the freestanding wall. These people talk and make noises as they carry their objects to and fro along the length of the road and back. Beyond the wall and the road is a fire that shines upon the objects that are being carried along the road and also upon

---

7    Indeed Plato refers to the rule of the philosopher-kings as enlightened and consensual (the subjects of a just *polis* consent to being ruled because it is enlightened) It is, nonetheless, kingly rule. See Book IV 431 b4 to e1.

the backs of the people who are chained to their seats. Further still from the fire is the mouth of the cave and ultimately the light of day, the sun. The prisoners of the cave do not see anything that is behind them. They see only the shadows that are cast by the things moving alone the top of the wall as well as their own shadows.[8] This theatre of shadows is all they know. It is their reality.

This is the basic structure in the myth of the Cave that Socrates relates to Glaucon (Plato's brother) in Book VI of *Republic*. The story is, if nothing else, a bit of a chestnut of western philosophy and has been interpreted, revised, reformulated, and reworked many times over. The general meaning of the myth's framework is not difficult to discern. We humans are the people who are bound to our chairs in the cave. Our ordinary knowledge of things is not "true" knowledge because it is based on the shadows we see on the wall in front of us. True knowledge requires that we first be freed of our bonds and turned towards things as they really are (the objects carried along the road and above the wall) as well as the light that shines upon them.

The process of freeing a prisoner in the shadow world and guiding this prisoner towards the light brings the Cave myth to life and is, for Plato, a tale of what philosophy and the philosopher are about. Once freed, the prisoner begins a philosophic journey upwards towards truth. It is a journey that ultimately takes him (or her) — the nascent philosopher — out of the cave to see the source of all that is known, namely, the sun. The journey upward is not easy, however, as the light is bright and requires getting used to while the things that are real look strange and less real than the shadows which the eye was accustomed to seeing and understanding for so long. Ultimately the freed prisoner becomes adjusted to the light and familiar with real objects rather than their shadows.

---

8    To further round out the "illusion" of the shadow world they also hear the echoes of what the people walking along the road are speaking and they attribute these sounds to the shadows as the bounce off the wall in front of them.

In time he comes to prefer the light and "reality" to the darkness and misleading shadows of the world that he left behind. It is at this point that the prisoner (now a full-fledged philosopher) is obligated (an obligation we will have reason to discuss further below as its source or its force is not so readily apparent) to go back down to the cave in order to help his fellow humans understand the truth about the shadow world they inhabit. Difficulties arise immediately because, in the philosopher's descent back into the shadows, he experiences the reverse of what he encountered in his ascent towards the light. The eyes are now unable to see very well in the darkness of the cave and what the returning philosopher tells the people in the cave about "real things" (the things being carried along the wall) strikes the literally unenlightened people as both strange and ridiculous. The philosopher sounds to his fellow prisoners more like a lunatic than a sage. Moreover there are others in the cave who have acquired power and influence because they are adroit at knowing and interpreting the shadows as they appear on the wall. These — let us call them shadow-adepts — look upon the (putative) mad ravings of our philosopher as efforts to usurp their power and authority, which, indeed, they are. For this reason these influential shadow-adepts work hard, and violently if need be, to put the trouble-making philosopher back in his place (seated and bound amongst the others). Should this fail they will more than likely resort to more violent measures and ultimately seek to put the trouble-making philosopher to death. And so the story goes.

That Plato intends his story to symbolize at least in part the troubled relation between Socrates and the Athenian *polis* of his time is clear enough. It is more to the point however to see that Socrates and Athens are themselves historical examples of a much more general concern of Plato's, a universal concern that the Cave myth is meant to convey in a compact albeit necessarily ambiguous manner. The Cave story, like many aspects of Plato's thought, occupies a unique place in the western imagination. It is, to begin with, one of the first (if not the first) mythical representations of how theoretical knowledge and the philosopher relate to society and is, in this way, hard to get beyond or dismiss simply out of turn. The Cave myth, in other words, occupies a kind of "meta" or initial position when in comes to talking about and understanding the human condition as one where theoretical knowledge about the world has (or can have) moral and political purchase. To write about or discuss matters of a moral and political sort in theoretical terms is to enter into the world of Plato's mythical cave in one way or another — even if the end result is to dismiss it. Let us look at that myth in greater detail to see why this might be so. I have chosen to break my discussion of Plato's Cave myth into four parts:

1. *The structure of knowledge — appearances versus reality.* Although we are inclined (because of our sophistication) to demur from so stark a concept of knowledge as one where a distinction is made between how things seem and how they really are, we might pause to ask: What is the alternative? If we talk about knowing, don't we automatically buy into some kind of structure of knowledge that makes distinctions between appearances and reality, and in this way buy into the Cave myth or something very much like it? There may be many ways to know things but the structure of truth itself (the interplay of appearances and reality) may be more singular.

2. *Periagoge (the turning).* In order to know the differences between appearances and reality one must be freed from what makes us see things only as they appear. According to Plato this freedom comes only when the person who is bound turns around fully towards things as they are and the light that shines upon them. The move from knowing the shadows (appearances) to knowing what is real is, however, more than a progression along a continuum of knowing and more than a correction that merely happens in the mind. The Periagoge is a total mind-body event.

3. *The Existential Question (the way up).* Here the question becomes: What drives the would-be knower of truth up towards "the sun"

and a greater understanding of reality? What keeps this would-be philosopher from turning back to the more familiar and comfortable world of shadows? This is a question of *eros* — specifically the love of wisdom.

4. *The Social Question (the way back down).* How and why does the knower relate to his fellow humans who are "unknowing" and who have not been freed and turned towards the light? This is a pedagogical issue but also and more immediately a political one. What obligation if any "makes" the philosopher go back down into the cave?

## The Structure of Knowledge

The epistemological components of Plato's Cave are easy to identify. They are: the shadows against the wall, the actual things that cast the shadows, the light from the fire and ultimately the sun that makes the whole thing work. It is part of the standard interpretation of Plato's Cave story to see in it (among other things) a mythical representation of Plato's epistemology, more specifically, his theory of the forms. In this theory it is the general form or idea of a thing that makes intelligible the particular versions of the thing that we experience and see in the world. The form or idea "man," for example, makes the individual men we know understandable as men. Another way to say this is that there are essences or ideas of things that stand behind or above the worldly, existential expressions of individual things that make it possible for us to know and refer to them as things of this or that sort. There are of course (all too well known) insurmountable problems with Plato's theory of the forms, most of which Plato himself acknowledged and articulated. It is however interesting to note that in the myth of the Cave we don't really find the theory of the forms as we normally understand it. There are the shadows and it is clear that these shadows represent the existential world that we experience, the world that the forms are meant to make intelligible. But the putative things as they really are, that is, the things that pass along the wall and cast the shadows, plus the light that makes these "real" things throw a shadow, are not so easily interpolated into Plato's so-called forms, or essences or ideas.

The things that are carried along the wall in Plato's myth are never identified as purely "ones" of a kind. We are not given to see, for example, someone carrying the essential dog casting the shadow for all existential dogs. Neither is the fire nor the sun portrayed as something that can be seen and known as if they contained or were somehow composed of the forms of all things. The usual conceptualization of Plato's theory of the forms is that there is the realm of being where the forms exist and the realm of becoming (our world) where particular expressions of these forms dwell — each individual thing participating in the idea to some degree and by implication "not participating" to some remaining degree. This has invariably led to (irreconcilable) "two-world" issues between the world of being (forms) and the world of becoming (the empirical reality we experience). In the Cave this two-world set-up is left behind for a one-world story with three components — the shadows, the things and the light.[9] This triad is not exactly the theory of the forms as we

---

9    Plato does set up what may initially look like a two world configuration because he represents the light in two ways. First as the fire, which is the source of the direct light that illuminates all things in the cave and, in this way, casts the shadows on the wall in front of the prisoners. Second as the sun, which is the source of all light and the ultimate end of the philosopher's ascent out of the cave. It is tempting to take these two "lights" — fire and sun — and assign them to their respective epistemological places in Plato's theory of forms. The fire is intelligibility in the world of appearances while the sun is the real and true (formal) intelligibility. The problem with this, as I noted, is that one is hard pressed to explain how the things that are carried along the wall and that are illuminated by the fire correspond to Plato's formal realities. If one presses the myth to give us this kind of interpretation it will break down. If I see the shadows of a pack of dogs running along the cave, there must be a one-to-one correlation between these shadows and the "actual" dogs (that is, the things being carried along the wall). One can say that both the things that people carry along the wall and the shadows they cast (and the fire that does the shadow trick) are all part of the world of appearances. OK then, but where are the forms for such

have come to know it; it is rather, I would argue, an epistemological framework that talks about knowledge in a more inclusive but also more generic manner.

What Plato is trying to show with the Cave story is what knowledge must look like, no matter what the epistemological fine print — including his own. The world appears to humans in a certain way; this world of appearances is channeled and defined by our biological make-up and by the cultural interpretations that are placed on the things our bodies experience. Implicit in Plato's Cave myth is the idea that the world of appearances hides as well as reveals. What it hides (and paradoxically reveals by virtue of this hiding) is the "reality-of-things" that (to use the idiom of the Cave) "stand behind" the appearances. This distinction between appearances and reality is central to the Cave story, and coupled with the condition of the cave dwellers, that is, that they are "normally" unable to look back, constitutes its most controversial assertion. The sun and the fire constitute the sources of intelligibility. While this role does not seem to present us with a notion as problematic as the Cave's other epistemological components, it is with the light — with the very assumption of intelligibility — where we can begin to understand some of the things that Plato's Cave intends to signify and explain.

Allan Bloom, in his commentary on Plato's *Symposium*, remarks that whereas Plato believes in a cave with shadows, things and an "outside" light, Nietzsche believes only in the cave.[10] In other words,

---

things as "all these dogs?" Is it all wrapped up in the fire or the sun? And what then is the distinction, within the world of appearances, between the shadows and the things along the wall? Are they two different kinds of appearances?

I think instead that Plato inserts the fire into the Cave myth so that he can draw the distinction between the source of intelligibility (the sun) and human intelligibility as such (things illuminated by the fire). The former can be contemplated but not known in a directly inter-subjective sense; the latter is what the philosopher and philosophy can bring to the human social-political equation and it is something that can (though not readily or easily) be communicated amongst ourselves.

10   *Plato's Symposium*, Benardate translation (2001) pp. 1-54.

for Nietzsche there is no light, or no outside light that is not itself part of the "shadow" world.[11] Bloom's rhetorical remark may not actually work if we think it through thoroughly, yet it is clear that what he meant to say was that for Plato the world is intelligible while for Nietzsche it fundamentally is not. Or, if you prefer, for Plato the world is intelligible only insofar as we discover its reality, while for Nietzsche the world becomes intelligible because men construct that intelligibility.

Setting aside the specifics of how we "know the world," the first challenge that Plato's myth forces upon us is this question of whether the world is intelligible in its own right or not. The myth as such does not answer the question; rather, it presupposes it and, in honesty, we might wonder how such a thing as intelligibility could be settled once and for all or even why we might bother to try. What kind of answer would ultimately satisfy so broad and fundamental a point? What would be gained if we were to answer this question above and beyond what our life experience tells us? There is at least some very immediate sense in which we "know the world." Perhaps it is true that the question is unanswerable because intelligibility is a brute datum of life — a given rather than a question to be answered, let alone understood. For Plato the notion that the world is intelligible is undeniable; or it is denied only because of ignorance, arrogance or duplicity.

To understand why this is so we need to understand the historical context of Plato's thought. If there is one theme that runs consistently through the body of Plato's work, it is the relation and the distinction between philosophy and sophistry. It is easy to miss this point because it is easy to read Plato as just another philosopher,

---

11    This helps explain the ontological link between the fire in the cave and the sun outside, as Plato clearly intends to argue that the fire is something that illuminates like the sun and is not something that humans put into place of their own accord. We have also already noted that there are epistemological reasons for having both the sun and the fire (otherwise the fire would be redundant and Plato should have just had the sun do the work of the fire).

albeit one who stands at the beginning of so many areas of western philosophical inquiry, and also as one who uses the dramatic
device of the dialogue to render his philosophy. There is for these
reasons the tendency to look upon the Sophists, the practitioners of
sophistry, as they appear in Plato's dialogues as simply the dramatic
foils and mouthpieces for competing and normally erroneous philosophical opinions. Socrates is Plato's sagacious spokesman for the
truth, and his (not so) cunning adversaries, the Sophists, are those
who abide and adhere to errant opinions. It is easy to forget that
for Plato (and Socrates) the Sophists were not a mere creation of
Plato's, but were a real presence in the Athens of his time. The stun-
ning claim of these Sophists, that they knew the good and that they
could teach it, was the starting point for Plato and his teacher *cum*
protagonist Socrates. From this starting point they argued that the
Sophists had not really taken the full measure of what they claimed
to know, let alone claimed to teach.

The Sophists held that man is the measure of all things, and for
this reason, knowledge of the world is always available to humans
simply because it is humans who actually produce it. Plato's objection to this position, by way of Socrates, was two-fold. First, if we
say that man is the measure of all things then it is only man that
can delimit and determine what counts as knowledge. If this is true,
then, according to Plato, knowledge is at its very foundation only an
expression of power — in the broadest and most fundamental sense,
what counts as truth is really what the strong (which is to say those
who have power) say it is — in other words, truth equals the interest of the strongest.[12] Second, regardless of whether we agree with
the Sophists or not, most people find it difficult if not impossible to
act as if they (*qua* man) were indeed the measure of all things. The
language and practices of knowledge and truth, according to Plato,
actually presume that knowing cannot be literally and totally man-
made and man-handled. To assume the Sophist position requires

---

12    This is exactly what Thrasymachus, the Sophist, says *Republic*, Book 1
338b.

a degree of cynicism and duplicity with respect to claims about knowledge and truth that even the Sophists found hard to maintain in their own practical lives — which in fact formed the thin edge of Socrates' wedge in all his discussions with the Sophists.

To return to Bloom's characterization of Nietzsche, the idea that there is only "a cave" is a sophistic position. If correct, it holds that knowledge is really just an expression of power. Plato's retort is that even if this position is correct it cannot be openly and publicly declared and defended, but rather must be left for the most part unsaid and hidden.[13] The latter is certainly true once a social-political context is added where knowledge claims are made and gradations of power exist. Although one may hold that man is the measure of all things — that there is "only" the cave — this is a position that cannot be openly acknowledged within an ongoing context of human interaction. In other words, people who know the truth (that man is the measure of all things) must lie to the (one presumes) far greater number of people who don't know it and who must as a result be told some tale about what is ostensibly the measure of all things.

It is my claim that to reject the sophistic position that knowledge equals power is to find yourself, by default, in a kind of world that can only be understood and subsumed under Plato's Cave myth. Having said this it is important to be clear about exactly what this claim includes. What it clearly does not include is a validation or proof for Plato's specific epistemology, especially as it is expressed in his theory of the forms. What it does claim is that the world is intelligible that this intelligibility forms the basis of our knowledge about it. It is emphatically an intelligibility that exists independent of any individual human mind (or use of force). At the same time this intelligibility is never fully revealed "in-this-world" but comes to us first through the appearances of things.

---

13    Let me note that even though I have used Bloom's characterization of Nietzsche, I am not necessarily crediting it.

If indeed the structure of knowledge is substantially as Plato portrays it in his Cave myth, then we are faced with this question: What can we know about the reality that lies behind the appearances of our world, not to say the source of intelligibility (the good), that Plato represents mythically and ultimately by the sun? We can start to answer this question by looking at Plato's understanding of the turning away from the shadows and towards things as they really are.

## Periagoge: The Turning

One question that arises frequently in Plato's political philosophy, even if not always explicitly, is (to speak woodenly) how does the first philosopher get made? The question comes up most notably when Socrates presents in *Republic* the notion of the philosopher-king including the educational regime that will make future philosopher-kings. If it is the philosopher-king who sets up the regime for future kings, then naturally one is begged to ask: How do we get this first such king? The implication is that Socrates was just such a "first" philosopher (if not king); though I would hasten to add that things are rarely that straightforward in Plato. The question of origins also arises when Socrates relates the myth of the Cave. Here again one is set to wonder, when a prisoner of the cave is freed of his chains, who is helping to make this emancipation possible? Again the implication is that Socrates — or someone very much like him — is the one. It seems, then, that we are compelled to ask: Who was Socrates and how did he come about?

I do not believe that Plato was interested in either setting up an historical regress — where we are never fully able to account for how a person might learn to turn from the shadows towards the light — or claiming that the only way this turning could happen was because of Socrates and only Socrates (though it is also clear that it is Socrates who affords Plato and his fellow Athenians the historical possibility of such a turning). There is rather an element of ambiguity and even fortuity in the notion that "someone" will help a prisoner of the cave free himself from his bonds. Most assuredly the helper is another human and not, for example, a god.[14] We can infer with some degree of assurance that this helper is yet another "at one time" prisoner in the cave. The implication is that, in theory at least, every human can become a helper and every human can be freed. The practical limitations to this universal emancipation are, however, immediate and all too real.[15] There are historical conditions as well as biological pre-conditions that will always circumscribe the number and likelihood of any would-be helpers (Socrates) and freemen (Plato). The Cave story is clearly meant to say that helpers and those they help (and that is to say those that can be helped) are always with us because this possibility is part of the human condition itself. Conversely, it is equally clear that Plato believed that the probability and number of helpers and turners was limited. There is of course no way (and perhaps no need) to even estimate what this probability might actually be at any one time or place. Plato offered the hope that we can see beyond the world of the shadows, but tempered this hope with the reality of how difficult and rare the realization of this hope might be.

It is important to stress the point that in the Cave story Plato is deliberately ambiguous about the particulars of how the turning comes about. This ambiguity is required so that we do not draw

---

14    This is in direct and pointed contrast to beliefs about Christian salvation which acknowledges Jesus Christ as both historically unique as well as divine.

15    Plato is not explicit within the Cave myth itself about the number of individuals who can execute the turning and once executed engage in the journey up towards the sun and then back down to the cave. By the way the story is told we can infer that the turning is not a common but rather a rare event. Plato reinforces this in Book VI 428 10 e5 where he speaks about the number of guardians in the just city as being "by nature," small in number. Exactly what Plato means "by nature" opens up an area of inquiry that is difficult to pin down. If we link this reference however with the myth of the metals it seems clear that Plato thought that the distribution of guardians *qua* philosophers would be like the distribution of metals — with gold being rare. See also Book VI 491 c.

the false conclusion that only Socrates can help us or only Plato can really be helped. The tendency in other words to see Plato as the *sui generis* recipient of enlightenment from Socrates (who is himself *sui generis*), and thus the authoritative spokesman for the true (Platonic) philosophy, must be avoided. The Cave story is not specifically about Socrates and Plato. It is about everyone — and no one.

It is evident that Plato meant to represent the turning from the shadows as something that could not be done by any individual acting on his own. It is clear that the prisoner could not free himself. And again, the ambiguity of who would help the prisoner allowed Plato to avoid questions about "the first helper" as well as establish that help was available, that is, implied within the human condition itself. We might offer as one interpretation of the Cave myth that it established the possibility of philosophy at the same time it argued that philosophy could not be conducted in isolation. Rather, philosophy occurs only with the help of others. The significance of this point will emerge as the analysis proceeds, for quite unlike his reputation, Plato did not believe and certainly did not fully condone the idea of the solitary, contemplative philosopher.[16]

Even before we examine what the turning is we see that Plato's story established, first, that the emancipatory logic of the Cave is a universal of the human condition, however mitigated that universality may be in fact. (And we will have further opportunity to examine this mitigation as we traverse the full arc of Plato's depiction of the ascent upward to the sun and descent back to the cave and its prisoners). Secondly, it established that "freedom" from the shadows (from the chains of ignorance) and the ascent to the light (towards knowledge) was something that happened between two (or more) people. This social dimension is also something that

---

16   It is equally clear that Plato understood and even experienced the pleasures of contemplative thinking. The final word on this however is that the philosopher cannot stay "deep in thought" but must, as we shall see, come back down to the cave and his fellow humans (see footnote 23).

will become more fully articulated as we delve further into Plato's myth.

Because Plato's philosophy is so readily identified with his theory of the forms and the idealism that this theory is believed to (rather strongly) imply, it is easy to overlook what the story of the Cave tells us about the turning towards things as they are and the light that shines upon them. What Plato called the *periagoge* is not a mere or simple intellectual conversion or movement. It is not a turning of the mind's eye so to speak from the wall and towards the light. Rather, the *periagoge* is a full turning around of the body from the shadows and towards the mouth of the cave. Our modern western point of view — seen through the lenses of an all too pervasive Christian mindset — is that Plato's rendition of what goes on in the mind was somehow distinct or detached (or at least detachable) from what goes on in the body. The temptation to drive this anachronistic Christian wedge into Plato's anthropology is admittedly bolstered by the putative "two-world" metaphysics of his theory of the forms. The simple yet compelling analogy goes something like this: The world of forms is to the mind as our existential world is to the body. In this way it becomes tempting to interpret the *periagoge* of the Cave myth as an escape from the body and the world of shadows into the mind and the forms.[17]

The only problem with this is that it is almost certainly wrong. Plato was not a Christian (even a "proto" one) and it is unlikely that he understood the human condition in the kind of stark ontological terms towards which we children of Augustine have been ineluctably drawn. There is rather a clear sense that for Plato there was no mind-body problem at all. Plato instead posited a tri-partite rather than dualistic psychology that we can roughly sketch as composed of mind, spirit and body (all of which compose the one natural psyche). This triadic theme (as we shall see in the next chapter) is in fact carried throughout Plato's thought from his cosmology (form

17    I will have more to say about this Christianizing of Plato when I talk about Plato's ideas about the structure of the world.

— life — matter) to his sociology (ruler — guardians — workers).
How these triads work and interrelate constitute an integral part
of Plato's political philosophy. The important point to note at this
juncture is that the *periagoge* of the Cave is fully dependent on and
consistent with Plato's organic conception of the human being; that
when a person is freed from his or her chains and is allowed to turn
toward the light and the things that are the source of the world of
shadows, this turning involves the entire person (the entire *psyche*)
— not just the "mind."

The immediate importance of this organic or "full-body" turn is
twofold. First, it alerts us to a psychology that is at least partially
foreign to how we normally think about things, especially as they
concern the intellect. The process of turning from the shadows to
the light involves the entire person and thus encompasses learning and doing things that are not just happening in the "mind," but
are happening throughout the body, soul and mind of the (would-
be) philosopher.[18] Second, the "full-body" turn warns us that this
is something that cannot happen without detection. Not only does
the *periagoge* require, as we have already noted, the help of another,
it also requires that others see that it is happening; it marks the
entire individual, not just his mind. That this was true for both
Socrates and Plato is evidenced by the trial and death of the former
and the retreat into the academy of the latter. What it might mean
in our own time presents an interesting question...though it is one
that, given our different mindset, we rarely confront and for reasons
I hope to make readily apparent.

A proper understanding of the *periagoge* sets the ground not
only for what needs to happen in order to become free of the shadow world, but also for what will follow. Again, if we insist on seeing Plato's story through the pure intellectualizing eyes of our con-

---

18    As we shall see further in the analysis, the very educational regime that
Socrates sets out in *Republic* is testimony to a view of the human condition
that draws into its ambit the entire person and pays respect to each of its
constituent parts.

ventional understanding of him, we are likely to miss this point or certainly to undervalue it.[19] Once freed, the would-be philosopher must begin his or her journey upwards to the light, and it is a journey that is neither easy nor particularly pleasurable for body, soul or mind.

*A brief digression (or not)*. The importance of an organic or integrated psychology as we find it in the Cave myth is also needed to give a compelling account of moral and political action. As Hume so rightly noted, reason by itself (and by implication the mind as reasoning organ) moves or causes nothing. If there is to be action or movement with a "responsible" human source, then that action or movement must stem from within the human, and its source must be something like what Hume called passion and what Plato identified as spirit. Of course to say this much is to say considerably less than enough, as the questions that fall from integrated psychologies of the Humean or Platonic sort are many. Not the least of which are: What is the relation between the organic self and the passions or spirit that move this self? And, how does this relation make it possible, or not, to denote one's actions as either virtuous or vicious? The specter that haunts any conception of human psychology of the naturalistic-organic kind is the specter of evil. Unlike Augustine's two-world rendition (where evil is essentially a corruption within the natural world — including and especially our body — and constitutes the location and occasion for evil insofar as man has fallen away from the God and the Good) or the Kantian hegemony of reason (where evil is ultimately an error or malfunction in judgment and/or thinking) a truly integrated psychology locates everything *in situ*, and so insofar as evil is a quality of the human world, it must also be the case that evil springs from the human condition and nowhere else...a bit of a daunting thought to say the least. I am not

---

19    It is interesting to note in this regard that Plato's founding of the Academy as a refuge from the very real dangers of Athenian politics should come to signify as noun, adjective and adverb a place of unreality that is made so by its over-reliance on thought above all else.

sure that either Plato (or Hume for that matter) ever delivers a sat-isfying answer to the nature and source of evil. Perhaps part of the problem is explained by the very fact that we have identified it as one. I suspect that a proper answer to the question of evil resides in a closer comparison and analysis between a naturalistic psychology such as Plato's and a transcendental psychology that is informed by the Christian notion of original sin.[20]

## The Existential Question: The Way Up

There are few axioms of our western culture (if I can be forgiv-en such a hackneyed expression). One such axiom is the idea that knowledge is good and indeed something of a good in itself (and it could very well be that this axiom pertains in some manner to all cul-tures). We might further attribute no small role to Socrates and Plato in helping establish this axiom within our own western culture. And yet, we find in Plato's myth of the Cave something that is less than a straightforward vetting of reason and the things it knows; for no sooner has our prisoner been freed and turned towards the light and the things as they are, that he becomes gripped by the desire to turn back and return to the comfort and familiarity of the world of shad-ows. And, why not? What is the passion, desire, or motive that drives the human being towards knowledge especially when acquiring that knowledge may be difficult and in some manner unpleasant (if not painful)? What would make our freed prisoner want to know more (want to go up to the mouth of the cave and see the sun)?

One of the texts that strikes many people as odd when they read Plato for the first time, and even puzzles and troubles them, is his dialogue about love, the *Symposium*. In our often-desiccated under-

20 Christianity as a set of ideas about the nature of man and the world will shadow our examination of Plato's thought as a kind of alternative competing "other." I will indicate towards the end of this examination that the perspective on Plato we have gained through our analysis of the Cave and how it relates to other modern political ideas and practices will also afford us a place from which to begin a reassessment of Christianity as well — a topic of future research.

standing of Plato there seems to be both little room and indeed little need for love (let alone erotic love). One is apt for this reason to interpret the *Symposium* as a mere incidental paean to erotic love set within a classical Greek context that is charged with homoerotic desire. Understood as such, the *Symposium* becomes viewed as a poetic *tour de force* that is not readily or easily related to our world or to what we have come to understand as Plato's overall political philosophy. If it tells us anything, it verifies that Plato is something of a prude, while it further exemplifies the methods and skills of Socrates the ironist and Plato the poet and not much more. The subject matter of the *Symposium* ultimately sounds, to most modern enlightened ears, like too much of the period. We tend to see it more as literature than philosophy, more a dated exhibit of classical Greek literature than the expression of timeless truth.

And yet, the ascent to the mouth of the cave would be incomprehensible — requiring some kind of *deus ex machina* — if Plato had not intended to argue that it is *eros* that moves the philosopher towards a greater understanding and the truth. Indeed the very word philosopher, "lover of wisdom," bears this out. But what does it mean to love wisdom? Does the lover of wisdom "love" in the same way as two human lovers love each other? In our culture (and perhaps in all cultures) the object of love, properly speaking, is paradigmatically another being. If not another human then surely some form of life — and the more sentient and the more human-like, the better. Mere material objects, not to say abstractions like the concept "wisdom," cannot be fully the objects of our love. Perhaps the *eros* that operates on the philosopher is for this reason less love-like and more like a desire or yearning. Yet this sounds an even more peculiar note to the modern ear than "loving wisdom." A desire or need for wisdom does not seem to fit well within the kinds of things that we normally desire or need — whether these things are objects like food and shelter or ideas like fame and fortune. It is true that the value of knowledge is hard to dispute and this is true not only in the sense that humans use knowledge instrumentally to their benefit (primarily to better acquire all the things they desire and need), but also in the sense that humans continuously wonder about the world around them and try to understand it. Some humans, regardless of culture, seem to take an interest in knowledge for its own sake. The key questions is: does this interest in knowledge, this desire to illuminate the wonders we have about the world around us, have enough substance and energy to propel and ultimately sustain the philosopher as he turns his back on the world of shadows and makes his ascent to the light?

On its face it would seem hardly even worth arguing the question whether knowledge is valuable or not, no matter what the context or conditions. After all, what is the alternative — ignorance? Why wouldn't any human want to know the truth? To move back to Plato's myth of the Cave: Why wouldn't any human, once freed from his or her chains, not want to see things as they really are and ultimately bask in the full light of truth? But that is precisely one of the problems the story of the Cave sets before us. It is important to note at this juncture that the pivotal distinction that makes the love of wisdom problematic is that the choice facing our freed inhabitant of the cave is not categorically a choice between truth and ignorance *per se* — between seeing and being totally blind. Rather it is between knowing the shadows and knowing the things as they really are. It is this existential distinction between what amounts to two kinds of "knowing" (expressed in the Greek terms *episteme* and *doxa* — truth and opinion respectively) that makes the *eros* of the philosopher both necessary but at the same time difficult to credit.

It is, as Hume argued, quite impossible to move humans simply by reason alone, so it is clear that in Plato's mythical movement up from the shadows to the light there has to be within humans (or at least some humans) the desire or passion for the truth of things as they are rather than as they appear to be; that the *eros* for truth is somehow built into the human condition. In other words there was no argument that Plato could make (even through the mouth of Socrates) that would have proved that humans desire the truth as his myth portrayed it. Rather the proof for this desire, namely, the *eros* for truth and wisdom, could only be found within the human heart itself — as is the case with all love, all *eros*. Our would-be philosopher, the person whose chains were broken and who turned toward the light, could find the strength and desire to ascend towards the truth because he was falling in love with this truth.

Several things can be said about the love of truth being inherent to the human condition. First, as we noted in the previous section, the turn towards the light is not a mere turning of the mind's eye but an action that encompasses the entire person — in commonplace terms, both body and mind. We can see more fully why this must be so, as we begin to understand that the desire to know things as they are (and the desire that keeps the philosopher on course) must come in conjunction with human passion and desire and not from reason or mind alone. In the Platonic idiom of things it is the entire "psyche" that is engaged in the love of wisdom.

Secondly, not only does the love of wisdom require the full person (the entire psyche), but again we have seen that the recognition and ultimate fulfillment of this love cannot be a solitary undertaking. A teacher, friend or even, let us say more *a propos*, a lover, must be involved in the ascent towards the light; so much so that it might be inferred that an integral part of the very object of philosophic *eros* is this other person or person(s).[21] The part played by

---

21 In the Platonic oeuvre there is an historical content that informs Plato's discussions of philosophy, and that content is Socrates the teacher and Plato the student. It is a mistake, however, to invest this peculiar historical happenstance with too much theoretical import. There is an asymmetry in the Socrates-Plato relationship that Plato duplicates in the Cave myth insofar as he identifies (or rather fails to account for) the person who frees the would-be philosopher and mentors him throughout his ascent. The question is (or so it seems) begged as to how Socrates or the mentor actually gets to be who they are. The matter of whom and how the first philosopher gets made so to speak is actually one that Socrates fails to systematically address in *Republic* when he talks about the philosopher-kings. The answer, albeit implied rather than stated, is that such a being is made

the emancipator in the Cave and Socrates in Plato's own education is paradoxically both incidental, because there is no blueprint for it (there is no necessity in the person Socrates), and essential, because a filial relationship between human beings is required to climb up towards the light while also being part of the very truth of things as they are (perhaps it forms the very core of this truth!). We are, in this way, brought back to Plato's *Symposium* and our third and final point.

It is certainly not a coincidence that Plato's myth of the Cave bears resemblances to the way that Plato constructed his *Symposium* dialogue where love is examined as an ascent up the ladder of love. As with the Cave, Plato arranged the different definitions of love given by the participants in an order that went from the most mundane within-the-world-of-shadows to the heights of seeing-the-truth; these are precisely the same starting and end points in the Cave. And finally, neither the freeman of the cave nor Diotima's lover of truth and beauty (namely Socrates) was left to simply bask in the glow of their accomplishment. The intrusion of the real world or, more specifically, the existence of "other people" was re-introduced into the philosopher's and lover's ascent. And so the philosopher as a lover of wisdom was compelled to face the existential question about his way of life: "You have seen the truth, now what?" "What will you do with it?" The ascent toward truth is brought back down. In the Cave, the philosopher descends back into the shadows. In the *Symposium*, a drunken Alcibiades crashes the drinking party; he represents a love gone wrong; a student who

---

sort of willy-nilly. The ontogenetic process (or perhaps more accurately the evolutionary process) that creates philosophy and the "first" philosopher is undoubtedly a valid question but it is different from what Socrates examines in his discussion of philosopher-kings. Such a question is, in its most literal and strictest sense, an empirical one which may not be fully answerable in theory. On the ambiguity of the "first philosopher," see Book VI 492e to 493a, also 496b.

succumbed to the shadows — a reminder that there was still and always will be work to be done.[22]

## The Social Question: The Way Down

There is one aspect of Plato's Cave story that virtually all readers and critics agree on; that is the part that refers to the philosopher's problems when he decides to return back down into the cave to teach his fellow cave dwellers about "things-as-they-are," including the light (and ultimately the sun) that shines upon them. Virtually everyone agrees that the ridicule and hostility the returning philosopher faces are meant to refer to the historical Socrates and his troubled and finally fatal relationship to Athens. The conventional wisdom goes even further, explaining that Plato was both condemning his fellow Athenians for rejecting the wisdom of Socrates and putting him to death, while also justifying his own "escape" from Athenian society into his putatively insular academy — a kind of world of the forms here on earth. That Plato was writing both an indictment of Athens as well as an apologia for the Academy in his Cave story is easy to see and hard to contest. A critical reader is nevertheless still forced to ask: Is this the whole story or even the most important part of it? What is dubious about this rather superficial reading of Plato's Cave myth is that it misses or begs one obvious point. Why would any philosopher (especially after being made aware of Socrates' fate) go back down into the cave? What makes the freed prisoners decide to return to the world of shadows? That this does not have a clear and obvious answer is the reason why we can begin to suspect that there is more than an indictment

---

22 Both the return back down to the cave and Alcibiades "crashing" into the *Symposium* can be seen as the dramatic mechanism that Plato used to indicate that philosophy and the *eros* that drives it forward were never "start-to-finish, "one-time events, nor was their success guaranteed. He turned them back in on themselves to indicate their circularity and their continuousness. We shall have opportunity to make reference to this circularity a few more times. See further Book VI 491 — 994 where Socrates eludes to Alcibiades as an example of the would-be philosopher gone wrong.

and apology in this final act of Plato's Cave myth. Indeed, it is the descent back to the shadows that provides a rationale for telling the myth at all and ultimately forms the basis of its significance for any audience, including our own.[23]

Let's return for a moment to our discussion about who the participants in the Cave story are. More specifically we can ask: Who is the emancipating teacher? Who is the prisoner that is set free? Looked at within the context of *Republic* it is clear that Socrates and Plato are in fact interchangeable as teachers (setting prisoners of the shadow world free), and that Plato and his students (including us, his readers) are also interchangeable as prisoners who are (or can be) set free by Socrates and Plato respectively. The broader and more significant conclusion that we can draw from this is that philosophers are both teachers and students within the process ("way of life" is perhaps the better expression) that is meant to set us free from the chains of common opinion and guide us upon a course towards the truth of things as they are, and ultimately, the source of truth itself...the light.[24] Philosophy as Plato conceived it then is a generational and ongoing way of life. There is attendant within this brotherhood of philosophy the next and obvious question of how it relates to the greater brotherhood of society itself. Here the strands of indictment and apology are mixed with the insight that there is a necessary relationship between philosophy and society, if for no other reason than because philosophers are themselves parts of the social order and ultimately members of the human race.

The standard understanding of Plato's view of the relationship between the philosopher and the larger social-political order was

---

23  That Plato means for philosophers to go back down see Book VII 519 c & 520 a; also *Republic* begins with Socrates *going down* to the Piraeus.

24  I caution the reader to remember that what Plato (or even we) can mean by the concepts of "understanding the truth" or "knowing the source of truth" are neither plain nor simple. In the way we commonly understand or speak about things like truth and knowledge, there is a sense in which neither the truth nor the source of truth can be known, or more specifically, enumerated. There is nothing that can be told or written that is literally the "whole truth." In this regard see Book VII 533 a5.

colored by his firsthand experience of Socrates' arrest, trial and death. This led him to retreat into the safe haven of the Academy from which he heaped withering (albeit often disguised) criticisms on the shortcomings of his countrymen, Athenian society and ultimately mankind as a whole. The underlying theme of Plato's philosophy on this view was that genuine human happiness and justice could not be realized unless and until they were informed and directed by a philosopher-king. Human society will be best ordered when it is ruled by philosophers and constructed so as to enable the succession of their enlightened rule. Rather than putting him to death, then, Athens should have made Socrates king!

The evident "unreality" or even downright absurdity of Plato's depiction of the philosopher-king, and ultimately the notion that the likes of a Socrates (or even Plato himself) would ever be put into a position to rule a political order (or teach a would-be ruler), is acknowledged in the myth of the Cave. The descent back into the world of shadows and the reception that the philosopher receives — the ridicule and suspicion that will ineluctably lead to grave consequences if the philosopher is not discreet — is the pessimistic twin of Plato's (putatively) sanguine thoughts about a regime that is ruled by knowledge. That the myth of the Cave was told by Socrates, literally within the very context of his presentation of the idea of a just regime that educates and is ruled by philosopher-kings, is for this reason strikingly paradoxical.[25] We might try to explain the paradox by saying that Plato was issuing a warning to any would be philosophers — "be careful, lest you run afoul of the authorities who treasure and defend the world of shadows." We might also say that Plato was attesting to the fact that just as the emergence of Socrates was historically unlikely — that is to say, the teacher who frees the nascent philosophers from their chains but whose own freedom appears to have no issue — so was the social

---

25  Indeed the Cave myth is the pivot point of the argument in *Republic* as it goes from defining and building the just political order (the first part of the dialogue) to taking it apart (the last part).

milieu that would accept the teachings of philosophy equally, if not more, unlikely. One is moved to conclude that the historical likelihood of the two ever coming together — a philosopher-king plus a society that will receive him — is virtually non-existent. In this regard Plato's just polity could never get started ... and doubly so!

That being said, however, we can see that the truly paradoxical aspect of Plato's philosophy becomes the intention that lies behind it: What, after all, was Plato's point? One is tempted to say it was that the ideals and ideas of philosophy regarding a just society cannot be realized within the world of practical politics and that, insofar as a just society can be known and appreciated at all, this can only be done within the confines of the Academy (or something very much like it) and by way of a communal philosophic discourse that is at once both guarded and hidden. This would certainly conform to the modern view of Plato, a view that achieves its apotheosis in Popper's indictment of Plato's philosophy as fundamentally hostile to politics (not to say a primer for totalitarianism!). According to this view, the descent back from the light down into the cave was meant to show that it couldn't or shouldn't be done except, one presumes, to find other "like" minded philosophic souls to free from their chains and guide up towards the light and into the Elysian fields of contemplative bliss that can only be found within the safe haven of the Academy. As for the rest of mankind they will never really know the truth, and even under the best of circumstances they can only hope to be ruled by people (namely philosopher-kings) who know what is right and good.

One reason why we are prone to interpret Plato the way we do is because it conforms so well to our own liberal-democratic views on philosophy and the modern university. We do in fact look upon institutions of higher learning, for example, as guarded and safe havens where ideas about human society can germinate and be cultivated rather than subjected to the harsh exigencies of the "real world." And we remain skeptical about all pure, unalloyed applications of moral and political ideas and theories to any real world order. Moreover, this is a skepticism that is fresh in our minds because of the latest experiment of this sort, namely Marxism — a philosophy that proved to be a particularly nasty form of utopian idealism.

Is Plato, then, just another (perhaps the first) utopian idealist? Of course, few if any philosophers would freely assume this pejorative description of their thought. But can we say that Plato failed to understand that theoretical ideas (like those promulgated in his dialogues about politics, and especially *Republic*) and practical actions (the flesh and bone of actual government) are not readily interchangeable without doing violence one to the other? Once again the standard view of Plato's thought is likely to lead us to the conclusion that he did in fact (mis)understand the world in a way that led him to vest ideas and theories with a reality that was both superior and at the same time directly applicable to practical human life. Isn't this what the myth of the Cave tells us? — *Well, not exactly.*

If Plato were indeed a utopian idealist, an enemy of politics, it seems to me he would have told quite a different story. Within the structure of the Cave story any form of social utopian idealism would require that ultimately (and at least under some circumstances) all the prisoners in the cave would be set free and brought up to the light. Even more tellingly, such idealism requires that the prisoners don't go back down to the world of shadows but in fact set about living within the world of things as they are — before the wall and in full light, if you will (in the Marxist lexicon, there would be perfect transparency).[26] Nothing in Plato's myth of the Cave suggests that this should happen; indeed it implies that it can't happen. Human society (within the idiom of the Cave) cannot exist "before

---

26   Even on this score Plato's peculiar rendition of social idealism would require that a distinction be drawn between the majority of people who have been freed from their ignorance of reality and the philosophers who, by virtue of having made the ascent all the way to the mouth of the cave, have a more complete knowledge of reality and have been instrumental (if not controlling) in the emancipation of others.

the (free-standing) wall." The philosopher's descent back into the world of the shadows is a return to the world he has never and (as long as he is alive and as long as he has a human *psyche*) can never leave. Human virtue and justice are finally things that happen in the shadow world even though they can and may be informed by an understanding of things as they are. They are not and never can be "things as they are." They are not and never can be "behind the wall."

Readers of Plato's *Republic*, starting even with Glaucon himself who hears it firsthand, usually are puzzled by the lack of practicality in Socrates' exposition of the just regime. Is the just *polis* that Socrates outlined (the regime of the philosopher-king) something that could be realized under any circumstances in our world? Socrates provided no definitive answer and indeed says that the just *polis* may be more a dream than a reality. If we look at the question alongside the myth of the Cave we can better understand why this is so. The just *polis* that Socrates detailed in *Republic* is an idea, more a reality than an appearance. In other words it is composed of things as they are, of things that are trucked along the top of the wall but are never actually part of the human, shadow world. The requirement that the just *polis* have a philosopher-king is better understood in these terms since it is only the philosopher who can properly interpret and negotiate the relationship between the things as they are and the shadows they cast. That the just *polis* that Socrates detailed is a kind of reality at a fever pitch — an event whose unlikelihood is matched only by its transience — draws us closer to understanding the subtleties that we tend to miss in Plato's thought. [27]

---

27  There are actually two types of questions about the "possibility" of the just city that Plato discusses in *Republic*. One type we can identify as being related to the specific parts of the just city, such as the separation of classes and the communal living arrangements of the guardian class. The other type concerns the possibility of realizing the just city in its entirety. Plato introduces this latter discussion in Book V 471 c when he has Glaucon bring Socrates up short in his discussion of war and the conduct

I would characterize Plato as neither an optimist nor a pessimist. It is true that reality disappoints us time and again, but to acknowledge disappointment is not an admission of pessimistic futility. Nor is the idea that one must carry on and try again and again to know and educate others in an act of blind optimism. It is rather a nod to the very structure of the human world. Plato's Cave story is about living in this human world and specifically about the part that philosophy can and cannot play in it. It is a story both of hope ... and of caution as well. (Or: It is a story of hope...but of caution as well.)

---

of the guardians in war (a discussion that is geared to the first question of possibility). He tells Socrates, in effect, that all these matters of practical detail are well and good but let us assume that they are settled and realizable. What, then, about the just city itself, can it exist? Socrates response starts with drawing the distinction between speech and action (theory and practice) and noting that things that may be realizable in speech may be difficult to realize exactly so in practice. Despite this difficulty Socrates argues that it does not mean that the things that are realized in speech are either less true or valuable. At the core of Socrates' response here is the argument that the just city founded in speech does not need to have to be realized in some past or future time to be a true model and depiction of justice (and entirely appropriate to the discussion at hand). Glaucon presses his point forward nonetheless and Socrates delivers the crowing paradox of *Republic* with his idea of the philosopher king. According to this idea, only when knowledge and power are united in one place (in the person of the philosopher) will the just city come into existence. This leads into a digression where Socrates defends true philosophy, and the philosophers who practice it, from criticisms about actual cases of philosophy and philosophers that don't seem to measure up to Socrates' depiction of them. It comes to an end in Socrates' argument that philosopher kings (or kings who are philosophers) are the only hope for realizing a just city and that there is nothing about this idea that makes it impossible (Book VI 499 b5). Socrates produces his final answer on the matter of whether the just city is possible or not in Book IX 592a where he states flatly that the decisive point is the idea or model of the just city (the city founded in speech) and not its historical realization. This assessment relates to my contention that the just city is a kind of reality at a fever pitch (see Book VI, 497 d5-10 for a hint of this). It is a reality that is so full of truth and being that it is difficult to realize let alone sustain over time. It is in this sense that it is more dreamlike than "real" — if by "real" we mean the practical political world we live in day to day.

# Chapter 2. Structure of the World

I have mentioned already how the conventional wisdom about Plato's thought tends to place him at the head of a tradition that, within our prevailing philosophical taxonomy, we usually label Utopian Idealism.[28] All forms of idealism, regardless of pedigree, tend to assert in some manner the preeminence of ideas over material reality. All varieties of idealism have tended to run aground, first because they cannot define what this "preeminence" of ideas over matter means, and second, because they cannot characterize how the ultimate, albeit evanescent, reality of ideas relates to the all too palpable reality of our mundane material existence. The

---

28 The arcane twists and turns of philosophic labeling are in evidence when we also note that Plato is often called an ethical realist. It is Plato's idealism, however, that informs his ethical realism insofar as ideas (actually, the forms and ultimately the idea of the good) are posited as the most real of things. In at least one use of the word "real," all philosophers are realists of a sort since all philosophers make assertions about reality and how it works. The common contrasting position against idealism is, in this regard, not realism but materialism.

metaphysical straightjacket of two worlds, one ideational and the other material, is a legacy we inherited, however, not from Plato *per se* but actually from thinkers — primarily Christian thinkers — who came some time after him. Yet, and ironically, "the two-world problem" haunts virtually any serious modern day interpretation of Plato's philosophy. The primary vehicle for rendering Plato as a "two-world" philosopher is located in the Christian worldview, perhaps best expressed and defended by its first major philosophical exponent, Saint Augustine. It was the argument and devoted belief of this influential and erudite Bishop of Hippo that we humans inhabited a cosmos that included two very different kinds of worlds, one material and the other spiritual. The former world, which he denoted as the City of Man, constituted the created material world we humans were born into and would one day leave when we died. The latter world, which he denoted as the City of God, constituted the eternal spiritual world from which humanity had fallen and to which, in death, our souls (if not our bodies) hoped to return. The theology of this two- world cosmos is complicated in detail and subject to a variety of interpretative slants. The broad sweep, however, is all too familiar. And it is the two-world cosmos that is invariably (and literally) read back into our understanding of Plato's philosophy.

Within canonical studies of western philosophy, Augustine is seen as having been greatly influence by neo-Platonist ideas and ultimately to have adopted and adapted a substantially platonic cosmology to his Christian theology. This Christian theology begins with a concept of a divine being that is all-powerful and all-knowing. Furthermore this "poly-omni" divine being has no beginning and no end in both a temporal and spatial sense — which, since Einstein, we have discovered pretty much amounts to the same thing. The complete and absolute perfection of the Christian God is admittedly not unlike the way Plato often conceived or discussed his view on ideas, especially the ultimate idea, that of the good; and, it certainly conforms to how we have come to view Plato's own metaphysical formulations. Furthermore, in both the Christian and Platonic renditions of the cosmos, the material world around us is decidedly derivative of and inferior to the ultimate spiritual/ideational reality. It is not difficult to see in Plato, then, some sort of prefigurement of the Christian cosmology. It should be noted, moreover, that Augustine's disagreement with Plato and his philosophical followers was not considered to be over the structure of the world as such, but over how much of that structure could be known by human reason without the grace of the Trinitarian God. What Plato did not know about humanity, according to the Christian view, was its fallen nature. He did not know (and really, from the Christian perspective, had no way of knowing it) that because of original sin, a basic flaw lay at the very heart of human beings that established an unbridgeable limit to human knowledge — not to mention moral and political rectitude. This limit furthermore could only be breached through faith in God's saving Word, which one could find only in the Christian Gospel; and, it most certainly could not be overcome by human reason alone. Our standard western interpretation of Plato's cosmology was further galvanized when that other preeminent Christian thinker, Thomas Aquinas, pronounced it too ambitious, while coming down squarely on the side of the more cautious and qualified Aristotle. We can better understand Aquinas' decided preference for Aristotle over Plato precisely because the former was less and not more "Christian" than the latter. Aristotle's' putative proto-scientific empiricism and less ambitious or hedged cosmological ruminations made him the ideal candidate for Aquinas' project to bring philosophy and theology into some kind of synthetic unity — with theology of course still in the controlling position. In Aquinas' view one could accommodate Aristotle far more easily into the Christian worldview than some one like Plato.[29] Nevertheless even Aquinas' beloved "philosopher,"

29   One might argue then that Augustine's more hostile view of philosophy was, by the same token, a function of his prior learning in and adher-

Aristotle, was not spared. The Protestant theologian Martin Luther (an Augustinian, of course), would find it necessary to repudiate philosophy in full, including its more cautious and accommodating "Aristotelian-inspired" variants that Aquinas had championed.[30] What Luther and other Christian reformation thinkers had come to realize was that the fault line between classical Greek thought as exemplified in both Plato and Aristotle versus Christian belief and theology was naturalism. Classical Greek thought is decidedly naturalistic while Christian thought is decidedly not — and indeed cannot be. The modern "enlightened" return to naturalism via critical philosophy and scientific investigation — whose seeds are planted in the late medieval and Renaissance periods and which in turn help explain Luther's full-fledged repudiations of philosophy — would seem, then, to signal a return to a worldview that is more conducive to understanding Plato's thought. Unfortunately, this is not quite so.

We might think that the twists and turns that Plato's philosophy experienced at the hands of his Christian descendants were ultimately remedied once the Renaissance and certainly the Enlightenment got under way and began to exert its critical influence on western philosophical thought. Although it is true that with the advent of modernity (let us say from the Renaissance on), critical and scientific thought processes were applied with greater and greater "success" to the theologically encrusted philosophies of the early church fathers (Augustine et al.) and their scholastic offspring (Aquinas et al.).[31] Certainly part of this success can be described as a "return" to an overarching naturalism, and by this I mean that

---

ence to Neo-Platonism.

30   Luther's theological rallying cry of "justification by faith alone" signals emphatically his repudiation of human reason as the guiding faculty of human existence which is, of course, profoundly contrary to the Classical Greek positions of both Plato and Aristotle... to say the least.

31   Just for the record, I am aware that "scholastic" thinkers like William of Occam and Marsilio of Padua are in fact part of the critical/scientific advance into modernity.

philosophers became less and less inclined to talk about worlds beyond the ken of reason and more and more inclined to talk about the cosmos as a self-contained (if not completely knowable) entity. However, the specter of Augustine's Man-God two-world dichotomy continued, and continues to haunt and influence the western philosophical imagination. Perhaps the clearest indication of that invasive (if not pervasive) influence is that we have tended to systematically misrepresent Plato's naturalism to this day. What do I mean by this?

The conception of nature that tends to prevail in the contemporary western mind might be best characterized as strictly monistic. Up until recently we might have even further described this monism as one that viewed the world in wholly material terms. As modern science has probed deeper and deeper into both the largest and smallest of things, however, the idea of the "material" world itself has begun to creak if not crack under the pressure. Nonetheless there remains the belief (if not the asserted certainty) among most scientists today that all of reality both big and small is made up of the same stuff and governed by one set of laws. What many non-scientists and even some scientists (in their non-scientific moments) find troublesome with the way we have come to characterize our cosmos, is that it seems to leave unexplained some of the (quite immediate) things we experience in the world and want most to explain. Among such unexplained "things," perhaps two very important are the thoughts that are in our heads (our self-conscious mind) and how or why we choose to conduct our lives in this or that way (ethical choice or agency). Of course, one can identify and characterize the suspected shortcomings of our monistic scientific understanding of reality in a variety of ways and undoubtedly identify shortcomings that go off in many directions; the point is that for many people... something is missing.

Faith, spiritualism, transcendentalism and the like are various ways that humans try to account for and put back into their lives the things that our modern scientific understanding takes out, over-looks or simply ignores. We can see in these efforts to move beyond the merely natural the continuing dynamic that Augustine identi-fied when he spoke about the respective cities of God and man. It is, moreover, this continuing dynamic between a naturalistic (*cum* materialistic) cosmology that claims (if not outright, then implic-itly) to include all that there is in the world, and our subjective experience of the human condition that seems to tell us otherwise, that leads me to conclude that an echo of Augustine's two-world cosmology is indeed still with us. It seems that when the modern enlightened sensibility (so to speak) critically banished the spiri-tual City of God from the arena of philosophic-scientific discourse, it failed to make the City of Man complete again.

The primary victim of our truncated scientific cosmology or criti-cal metaphysic has been our moral and political understanding of the human condition. A great many people, as already noted, tend to resolve their differences with our prevailing enlightened sensibil-ity by turning towards and believing in things that are quite liter-ally out of this material-scientific world. These otherworldly things, insofar as they are believed, are held to be indisputably true because there is no way to rationally dispute them. One either believes in them... or not. The actual mechanisms of belief — which is to say how one comes to have faith in this or that otherworldly thing — are many and can be quite complex. For our purposes such differences are not important. What is important is that, from a philosophical point of view, once you move beyond the "natural material world" and into other forms of reality that are, by definition, fundamentally unknowable to human reason, you find yourself back in some kind of Augustinian "two-world" cosmos.

Plato's naturalism, I contend, does not come equipped with this Christian *cum* Augustinian "two-world" baggage. The cosmos for Plato is, as it is for modern science, a world that is one and self-con-tained. The difference is that Plato's conceptualization of nature is (for lack of a better term) more differentiated; it holds within it all that humans know and experience. Specifically, Plato's world is a world (and again, one must search for the right words) that consists of matter, spirit and mind, where matter equals the stuff out of which the world around us is made; spirit equals the energy or force that moves matter; and mind equals the principle of its intelligibility (knowledge and time come from this). The modern scientific world deletes mind (quite literally) from its famous cosmological equation of matter and energy ($E=MC^2$); and, it is this deletion that helps distort our understanding of Plato's thought — at its very root. Within the modern scientific worldview our knowledge and experience of the world remains profoundly under-explained.

Even if we agree that it is accurate to say that our concept of the world remains incomplete because we fail to account for or acknowledge mind (or some such "thing") as a part of the world, we are regrettably even less prepared or equipped to rectify this deficiency in our worldview. We might wish to promote the project: "explain mind" or "put mind back into the cosmos," but we are, at least for the moment, quite unable to give it very much substance. Within the modern scientific outlook — an outlook whose lock on naturalism is hard to break out of — there is no way to explain mind except to reduce it to some complex of matter and energy. There is no way to grant mind an ontological status that is not ultimately dependent on the matter and energy we assert it is made from and powered by (which is respectively the brain and its support system, the body). Literally the brain-body complex is all we see because it is all we are equipped to see. So why not conclude that our good friend Plato simply got it wrong, that because of his lack of scientific sophistication (a sophistication we have since gained) he wrongly thought that mind was a fundamental part of the cosmos? Why not conclude that "mind" is instead (and at best) a phenomenon of the physical human brain — and at that, a rather local phenomenon in our vast cosmos?

And so for most of us, modern naturalism cannot make contact with the naturalism of Plato. In and of itself this may seem mostly unproblematic. This would be true (and is more true with the likes of Aristotle) were it not for the fact that Plato's political philosophy is both tightly bound to his version of naturalism, while at the same time profoundly intertwined with our own ethical and political ideas. This means that when we question Plato's naturalism (that is, when we question his concept of the structure of the world) we also put into doubt his ethical and political ideas and, by some significant measure, our own political and ethical ideas as well. Again, this may not seem overly problematic — especially for all the many critics of Plato's ethical and political philosophy. I would argue instead that it is significantly problematic, in a way that is (ironically) so deeply rooted as to be nearly invisible. How is this so?

There is in Plato's *Republic* the famous isomorphism of man and *polis* that Socrates deployed to illuminate and elucidate both the one and the other... going back and forth from the larger to the smaller, the smaller to the larger, as the argument required. This isomorphism is easily stated: the *polis* is man writ large; man is a *polis* unto himself. The components of this isomorphism are also readily identified if not so easily understood. In the *polis* there are the rulers, the guardians and the workers, and these directly correspond in the individual person to reason, spirit and appetite. Critics of Plato's political thought, especially as it is expressed in *Republic*, are quick to point out both the inadequacy of the isomorphic components (they don't seem to cover all that there is in either a *polis* or a human) as well as the strained or overwrought quality of the isomorphic assertion itself. Although there might indeed be analogous elements between human beings and the political associations they build and inhabit, there does not seem to be, upon closer and careful analysis, anything like the tight isomorphism that Plato's Socrates articulated in *Republic*. Indeed the isomorphic comparison seems to suffer equally in both directions: a *polis* hardly looks or acts in anything like the organic fashion that one would expect to find in a human; while a human is not so easily divided and understood as a combination of three distinct functional components. The sympathetic reader is perhaps at best inclined to interpret Plato's isomorphic comparison between man and *polis* as only a heuristic device, not a description of reality.

However one chooses to interpret Plato's isomorphic comparison between humans and political forms, it is important to remember that a strong element of irony pervades Socrates' discussion of justice in *Republic*, especially and including what he means when he formally identifies individual humans with political entities. One element of this irony is that the isomorphism of man and city cannot be literally true if by "literally true" we mean true in our practical, experienced world; that is, what in Plato's Cave myth is designated as the world of shadows. Words like reality and truth, as we noted in the previous chapter, have a double meaning for Plato because they can be applied in two different ways (really in two different "directions"). They can refer to both what is going on in front of our eyes and what is going on behind our backs. Irony and myth are important mechanisms for navigating and communicating this bi-directionality, and become essential devices for talking about what most often cannot be said explicitly or directly. The empirical truth or falsity of Plato's man-city isomorphism is for this reason a question that is somewhat off the mark.[32] Trying to sort out and understand how two ways of knowing and two kinds of "reality" are

---

32    The entire purpose of the man-city isomorphism comes to a climax in Book IX of *Republic*. Here Socrates uses the larger, more readily observable typologies of unjust cities to demonstrate that not only are they unjust but unhappy as well. This helps him "prove" that the same is true for the corresponding (isomorphic) unjust individuals (which is the ultimate issue Glaucon wants answered, that unjust people are not only unjust, but unhappy as well). The argument reaches its apogee in the person/city of the tyrant where the isomorphism of man and city collapse into one. The mirror image of the tyrant, of course, is the philosopher king. The elegance of this argument is breathtaking as philosopher king and tyrant stand at opposite ends of an "order — disorder" continuum, with the teaming variety of political reality playing itself out in the middle.

and are not related becomes a central component to understanding how Plato's moral and political thinking operates. Moreover, the central figure in working out the exchange between these two realities is the philosopher who acts as a conduit between them. When Socrates united these two "realities" in the concept of the philosopher-king — what I called in the previous chapter reality at a fever pitch — he brought the isomorphism of human and city to its inevitable yet paradoxical conclusion. This concluding irony indicated masterfully the practical impossibility of ever successfully and finally collapsing the two "realities" of the Cave into one, in other words of ever effacing once and for all the distinctions and differences between appearances and reality.

It is easy to see why Augustine would, and ultimately could, adapt the Platonic "doubling" of reality and truth to a Christian cosmology that believed that the material world we experience through are bodies had somehow fallen from the fundamentally true and unknowable reality of God. Plato's ironic notion of the philosopher-king, however, got replaced in Christian theology by the mystery of the Holy Trinity where an inscrutable God holds dominion over all that exists. Augustine subverted Plato's irony and solved his "problem" as to whether the philosopher-king could ever exist by replacing him with God in Heaven, a being that not only exists but is the source of everything that does exist. The replacement of the philosopher-king with God also shifts the matter of Plato's isomorphic comparison of man and city to a different location. In historical terms this new "place" became the Christian church, or essentially any person or institution that claimed to know how to interpret and implement the word of God in this world. And again the irony of making this isomorphic comparison becomes completely lost and replaced by the literal, albeit mysterious, identity of our souls with God in the kingdom of heaven — the City of God. That this did violence to Plato's thought, violence we seem unable to correct or mend, can be seen in each of the prevailing myths used to explain the structure of the world — the Christian Garden versus Plato's Cave. Whereas Augustine believed in the Fall of Man, Plato argued for an ascent from the cave. A further bracing irony: what precipitated the fall from grace and initiated the turn and ascent in the cave and upwards to the light was one and the same thing — knowledge!

It is no accident that we members of the Christian West — of whatever stripe, and especially, I hasten to add, modern scientists — think of ourselves more as children of Adam rather than as prisoners in Plato's mythical cave. We are for this reason most apt to think of ourselves as less ambitious than Plato in our quest to know the truth. We assume that our epistemological goals are more in tune with our limited rational capacities. Plato, I have argued, becomes the audacious even arrogant thinker we find in our textbooks of Western Philosophy, because we read and interpret him in a context that makes him appear audacious and arrogant. Plato is seen to make claims about knowing things we have concluded either can't be known or don't exist... which in the Augustinian worldview amounts to the same thing. Let's look to that worldview again and make quick with how the entire confluence of western philosophic thinking since Augustine folds right into it in one form or another.

Augustine as we noted divided reality in two. There was according to Augustine the mundane world we live in and the spiritual world in which we participate (in some fashion) by virtue of our soul. As previously noted, the theology of this two-part world can be quite elaborate and has many different variations, some more significant than others, especially for those who believe in, defend and criticize them. However, for my purposes these differences are unimportant. What is significant is that Augustine took what was for Plato essentially one world and divided it into two quite distinct ones.[33] Most importantly, Augustine took what made the

---

33   Even though I have spoken of things behind and in front of the wall it is important to note how the Cave myth Plato maintains the integrity and unity of one world. The difference for him between things and the shad-

world intelligible and located it in a prior (and timeless) spiritual world whose workings human reason is unable to fathom. The differences between Plato and Augustine on this score are obscured by Augustine's neo-Platonism, for he started a tradition of Christian thought that incorporated into its conception of salvation what looked like Platonic imagery and concepts. The myth of the Cave accordingly became a prefigurement of the ascent of the soul up to God (the sun) with Socrates playing the part of Christ. The problem with this apparently happy union of Christian and Platonic imagery is that they simply don't inhabit the same kind of world. The structure of Plato's world contains the source and substance of knowledge within itself, primarily in the concept of mind (*nous*), and insofar as Plato had a concept of God (what in the Cave he represents as the Sun), it is best understood as pure mind, pure intelligibility and certainly not a "being" like the Christian God. This difference is critical to understanding Plato's moral and political thought, because for Plato it funded the possibility and potential validity of any and all moral and political discourse. Plato's isomorphic comparison between man and city when seen in this light was based upon an even more fundamental comparison or isomorphism — that of nature itself, first with man and then, by way of man, the city. All three entities consisted of isomorphically related components — roughly: matter, spirit and mind. The existence of these isomorphic connections between nature, man and city were in turn all based on the centrality of the human condition to Plato's philosophy. To say the matter differently: Plato's naturalism was one that included and understood human beings and human society in a way that made them central to his conception of how the world was structured. This is altogether unlike modern scientific naturalism, where self-conscious human beings and the societies they build and inhabit are both derived from the material world and are seen as

---

ows they cast (between appearances and reality to say it another way) is the direction in which the human being is looking, not the world he/she is inhabits.

fundamentally inconsequential to the workings of the universe as a whole. Modern day scientists, for these reasons, are apt to interpret Plato's brand of naturalism as excessively anthropocentric, as quaintly granting far too much to humans and their world when it comes to understanding the universe in its entirety. The standard explanation of Plato is once again easily wheeled into place. Plato, like any pre-enlightened thinker, simply placed too much emphasis on human beings while our wise post-enlightenment sages have all come to know that man is not the center of the universe...not even close. Our world is instead the world of $E=MC^2$ and is, as such, a mindless world. Yet it is precisely by virtue of this mindlessness that we find it difficult — and to be completely frank, impossible — to explain ourselves and the societies we have built and live in. The prevailing "scientific" assumption is that our present limitations in understanding the human condition are entirely a function of and shortfall in scientific knowledge that is yet to be acquired. Greater understanding about how the brain works, which is to say how it causes thought, and how evolution organizes human life and society (regardless whether this dynamic is driven by genetic or species forces, or both), will ultimately unlock the mysteries of how we humans fit into the vast overarching $E=MC^2$ cosmos.

And so, I return again to what makes human beings restive about modern scientific naturalism, namely that it falls short (far short) of explaining some of our most immediate experiences, primarily self-consciousness and moral agency. While it is true that there is no reason to assume that things like consciousness or agency require any explanation that is anything more than what science has so far given or will give us, it is also true that such explanations mean consciousness and agency are phenomenal realities that are unalterably not what they seem. This presents a truly ironic twist to Plato's myth of the Cave. In the modern scientific version of Plato's myth we are like prisoners looking at shadows on a wall... but there is no turning around. Indeed there is more than that. We human prisoners cannot turn around and see our true reality because we have no such reality *qua* human to see. Insofar as modern science understands the world, it does so by standing outside of it. It looks at the cave from the outside. This third party perspective forms the very basis of scientific objectivity. Science so conceived, however, cannot fully capture the entire structure of the world because it cannot bring the *knowing* human mind (the objective observing eye) within its own ambit. It is this gap in our knowledge that Augustine and all non-naturalists fill with some kind of transcendent reality that provides the foundation for knowledge (in the final analysis this is what the Garden of Eden story is all about). It was Plato's position, I contend, that any truly comprehensive naturalism must look upon the structure of the world as containing not just matter and energy, but also mind, and this means specifically the knowing human mind. It is this inclusion of mind within the structure of the natural world that informed Plato's ethical and political thought and, more to our point, it is the echo of this inclusion that we still hear when we start to talk about what it means to live well, to live a happy life in a just society. Modern scientists are prone to cut any kind of ethical discourse of this kind short and hand it off to other scholars in fields of inquiry like religion, philosophy, politics — as if these "other" scholars conducted their business in some kind of existential arena that exists, by special scientific dispensation, in some mysterious part of our world. Of course, there is no mystery about this once we recognize that these other fields actually exist in a phenomenal (shadow) world that is ultimately animated and driven by forces it faithfully registers but in no way directs or controls. The cynical secret of modern science is that the world happens to us and that our moral and political concerns are fundamentally misguided. Plato argued (via Socrates' challenge to Sophism) that this degree of cynicism was absurd at its root because it could not be logically defended in a discussion between two actual thinking and acting human beings. If Plato's argument was correct we are then faced with a choice among three prevailing myths — the Cave, the Garden, or...E=MC². In reality, we have tended to vacillate between E=MC² and the Garden and bury the Cave beneath this vacillation. This choice has deep implications for how we think about the moral and political universe we inhabit. In the next chapter we will examine some of these implications as we examine some of the topics that tend to separate Plato's ethical world from our own.

*Précis:* The claim that Plato did not subscribe to a "two-world" cosmology, one material and one transcendental, and thus can better be described as some kind of naturalist or monist (like Spinoza, for example), is, as I have noted already, not how Plato is normally understood. I have further claimed that it is Christianity that adds the other "transcendent world" to Plato. These seem dubious claims at first precisely because Plato often talked about such things as the soul being immortal and (somehow) distinct from our (material) bodies. Indeed the final chapter of *Republic* includes a myth about the process whereby souls leave their old bodies and choose new ones. There are a host of complex philosophical, not to mention philological, issues involved with questions such as this, but my claim that Plato was a naturalist or a monist is a rather general one and not overly sensitive to these complexities. I conclude that regardless of whether Plato truly believed souls were detachable from bodies, or whether he believed that ideas are more real than the material things that somehow participate in them, I do not find that he (or Aristotle for that matter) ever explicitly asserted that there are two separate worlds — two worlds that are in a significant way broken off from each other. This, however, is precisely the Christian view. For Christians of virtually any stripe there is one world that is spiritual and everlasting, and another that is material and mortal (with a beginning and end).[34] This cosmological difference between

---

34    It should be noted, however, that for Christian theology the ontological status of these two worlds is a constant source of debate and controversy. The problem starts with the poly-omni nature of the Christian God

Christian dualism and Plato is even more significantly reflected in their different conceptions and claims about human knowledge. However many pieces and parts there were to Plato's epistemological puzzle, he never segregated them into completely disconnected entities. The Cave myth itself details a continuous albeit articulated world where humans turn and move about from the shadows and up to the good and back — continuously. The Christian cosmology posits two entirely separate realms, each with characteristics that are not only distinct but also arguably opposed to each other (one eternal, the other time-bound), and each requiring distinct ways of knowing — by revelation and by reason, respectively. I have argued in this chapter that Plato's naturalism, primarily by way of neo-Platonism, was hijacked by Christianity (Augustine being the main culprit) and transformed into the transcendental idealism that is nowadays so readily attributed to him. I further explained that this attribution is aided and abetted by modern "post-enlightenment" thinking (primarily modern science and specifically physics)

---

— a God who is omnipresent, omniscient, omni-powerful — and ends with trying to explain how and in what way this omni-God relates to the natural world, especially given that this world is a world of change, difference and limits. In other words, and more pointedly: How is the Christian idea of God squared with such things as death, free will and (especially) evil? It can be noted that part of the impetus for Augustine's formulation of the City of God and the City of Man was the Manichean notion that the cosmos was actually composed of two ontological grounds, one good and one evil. In response Augustine devised an ingenious solution that refused to grant final ontological status to what appeared to be limits on God's nature. Instead, apparent limitations to God's poly-omni character were viewed as deficits — a degradation or falling away from being and thus partially non-ontological. The similarity of this notion to Plato's own cosmological ideas, especially as these reached Augustine by way of neo-Platonism, is undeniable and has already been noted. The telling difference between Plato's and all Christian cosmologies, however, is conveyed by the prevailing myth that each uses to illuminate them — the Cave versus the Garden of Eden. Knowledge animates the movements of the Cave, whereas knowledge is a prohibition and ultimately a curse in the Garden. Whatever the ontological status of our world is for the Christian, it is clear that another (more perfect and complete) world exists apart from this one, and that the only way to get there is by divine intervention (revelation, redemption, salvation) and certainly not knowledge gained by human reason.

which does not understand let alone credit the kind of "physics" (or conception of nature) that was needed to underwrite Plato's brand of naturalism. To the modern scientific or critical eye, once it confronts concepts like soul or mind it hands down the indictments — dualist, idealist, transcendentalist — and the guilty verdict: fallacious.

The differences between Plato's and Aristotle's plight on this score are instructive. Both Plato and Aristotle, I have claimed, believed in one natural world, that they were both monists. Moreover, both Plato and Aristotle (and in some sense even more so Aristotle) subscribed to a physics and cosmology that have since been fundamentally discredited by modern science. Yet, it is Plato who is labeled the transcendental idealist and Aristotle the empirical scientist *avant le mot*. There are undoubtedly several reasons for this. Plato tended to rely heavily on ideas and reason; Aristotle in turn worked to gather evidence and draw conclusions based upon it. I think that another important element in our assessments of these two thinkers, however, involves how closely they linked their respective physics and cosmologies to their political philosophies. Indeed, as the present chapter argues, the link for Plato was necessary and direct. *Republic* assumed that the world was structured in a certain way (*pace*, the three-part isomorphism that applies from man, to city, to cosmos). Aristotle's ruminations on ethics and politics, on the other hand, purposely held the cosmos (and the physics behind it) at arm's length. Although politics and ethics for Aristotle required that the world be in some measure orderly, logical and knowable, he significantly mediated and guarded the actual contours of that measure. This disconnection between physics and politics has helped Aristotle's reputation as both a political philosopher and a natural scientist (and it is a separation that is in fact mirrored in the creation of our own generic academic silos: Philosophy and Natural Science). For Plato, on the other hand, it has tended to distort and discredit both his politics and his cosmology. Part of the problem here, as this chapter tried to point out, is that we see Plato through Christian eyes (and this is true even when these eyes claim to be critical or scientific). This Christian distortion has made it difficult (if not impossible) to critically assess Plato's strong claim that politics and the structure of the world are (and need to be) closely linked.

# CHAPTER 3. BAD PLATO

Our common depiction of Plato as the paradigmatic "ivory tower" idealist philosopher is joined by the equally common interpretation of Plato's political philosophy as prudish, paternalistic, or worse. It is not difficult to see why this might be so. The "best" political regime that Socrates outlines in *Republic*, and even the secondary ones that are ostensibly sketched out in both his *Statesmen* and *Laws*, strike most of us as political orders that are harsh and joyless rather than as ones that would produce anything like the kind of human well-being and goodness that we would normally want and expect. Plato's argument in every one of his "ideal" cases, however, follows directly from the idea that "the people who govern" actually know to some very strong degree what they are doing. In other words, the rulers know what makes people happy as well as good, and the laws and policies they implement and administer are designed to achieve this result — however prudish or paternalistic they may seem to our modern eye. As noted already, the underlying and determining irony about Plato's political philosophy, and especially his thoughts about ideal political orders, is that the union of knowledge and power that it presupposes is extremely problematic because it is a union that is both highly unlikely and largely unstable for a whole host of reasons — most of which Plato details in the latter half of *Republic*. The use of irony and the recognition of how challenging the equation of knowledge and power is within any practical world setting are central to Plato's political philosophy, and certainly they are key factors in interpreting his description of any of his "ideal" political orders and most unquestionably the one he presents in *Republic*. When this complicating irony and the implied challenges it sets up are not given full measure — as many modern interpretations are wont to do — then Plato truly becomes the prudish, authoritarian and joyless philosopher that we have come to know him as. I must add that this is an odd not to mention unjust legacy for a thinker who wrote so beautifully and passionately about truth and goodness.

I plan to examine in this chapter four specific topics that have contributed to Plato's bad reputation. These topics are freedom, equality, public truth and art. Some of these may seem obvious to the reader, and others not so. Let me briefly explain what each will involve before I proceed to examine them each in greater detail:

*Freedom.* This concept is generally considered to be primarily a modern one, and as such one that is not easily found or read into the texts of an ancient thinker like Plato.[35] The reason for this absence is further thought to be based on our prevailing conceptions of the individual, and more specifically on our belief that human fulfillment and happiness is first and foremost something that happens on an individual basis. Ancient thinkers such as Plato, by contrast, are believed to have looked upon individuals more through the eyes of the socio-political orders or communities of which they were a part, rather than as self-determining not to say self-fulfilling indi-

---

35   Indeed Plato is often inclined to refer to freedom in rather pejorative terms as a kind of license and disorder, see Book VIII 557c -563e.

viduals. The matter is complicated to say the least. Still, however we choose to cut the conceptual cloth of individual freedom, there is clearly a sense in which Plato's moral and political philosophy appears to neglect the matter in a way that makes modern sensibilities anxious. This neglect or absence is indeed there, but once again I think our common understanding of Plato makes us mistake it for something it is not and, more importantly, makes us blind to aspects of Plato's thinking that speak directly to things we find wanting in our own moral and political thoughts and actions. We shall see, for example, that the stiff-fingered handling of ideas such as "public" and "community" by our modern liberal-democratic ideologies are the flip side of Plato's "neglect" of freedom.

*Equality.* While Plato's thoughts on freedom tend to be absent or at best implied, his ideas about equality are a different matter altogether. It is generally believed that Plato's position on the matter of equality is expressly elitist and paternalistic — a belief born out most emphatically by his depiction of the philosopher-king in *Republic.* This belief is also bolstered by his overall notion that people differ in terms of their talents and capabilities, and that within a properly ordered regime, these differences are accurately reflected in an articulated distribution of power and status so much so that in the truly ideal political order, talents and their (unequal) distribution match up perfectly. Of course, like freedom, the concept of equality is not a simple one and has many different and controversial meanings. Once again I will argue that, as with the concept of freedom, our thoughts about where Plato stood on the idea of equality are passed through a series of modern lenses that tend to filter and distort rather than clarify what these thoughts are. Let me advise from the start, however, that it is not my intention to transform Plato into some kind of closet or backdoor liberal democrat. It is, quite to the contrary, my intent to partially subvert and radically reposition the liberal-democratic notion of equality.

*Truth (and lies).* Closely linked to Plato's thoughts on equality is his position on public truth telling — or to put the matter in its more negative form — lying. The strongest example of this link is in *Republic*, where Socrates describes how the philosopher-king (and his guardian cohorts) develop and promulgate a myth about how humans are made of different metals (for example, gold-silver-brass and iron), to explain and ultimately justify the differences between people within a political order. Socrates calls this myth a "noble lie" because, though it is not strictly speaking true, it is based on a truth that (so Socrates told his listeners) could not be publicly spoken because it could not be properly (or publicly) understood. Setting aside the particularities of this particular example, the very notion of public lying of any sort does not sit well with most modern political ideologies, and especially not the prevailing liberal-democratic ones where a condition of complete transparency has tended to form the limiting ideal of public discourse. Again, I will argue that our enlightened prejudices have made us interpret Plato's ideas in a way that fundamentally misrepresents him as concerns the topic of public truth telling; moreover, it also deafens the modern ear to the more subtle (and ironic) meanings that Plato tried to relate as concerns the matter of truth within an ongoing political order.

*Arts.* Plato's ideas about the relationship between a well-ordered political community and art are again ideas that are not easily digested by the modern enlightened stomach. Their most extreme expression is, once again and not surprisingly, found in *Republic* where Socrates outlines a program of artistic control and censorship that appears, to say the least, bracing — especially for people who have lived in an era such as ours where totalitarian regimes have indeed exercised a high degree of control over the full range of liberal, fine and practical arts. It is perhaps this depiction of how the just city should handle the arts that contributed most to the  notion that Plato is both an enemy of freedom and an ancient champion of a thought process that, given the technical resources of the twentieth century and beyond, has issued into the realities of totalitarian-type regimes.[36] In some sense Plato, by way of Socrates, is guilty as charged. The charge can only be made to stick, however, if the controlling condition is met. This condition is the unlikely (not to say unstable) event when knowledge and power are united in the person of the philosopher-king. Our inquiry into the myth of the Cave has already tried to suggest that this unity is part of a larger existential picture that warns against the currently received interpretations of Plato's political philosophy. Plato's position on the relation of art and the just political order (as well as on freedom, equality and public truth) form part of that larger picture. Indeed, Plato's attack on art may be seen as the crowning irony in the rich brew of irony he served up in his Socratic dialogues — that are (not incidentally and altogether ironically) dramatic and beautiful works of his own artistic hand.

Let me digress briefly to explain how I am going to deploy a rather broad conceptualization that will help me better discuss the four topics I have just identified. Although the political landscape of our modern world is populated by a variety of political systems and the ideologies that underwrite and defend them, there is within this variety a broad band of systems and ideologies that I will call the liberal-democratic complex. This broad band of political forms and ideas can be seen to exist along a continuum that is bound on one end by extreme anarcho-libertarianism, and on the other by utopian-communism. Whether one chooses to include

---

36   Plato's discussion about art in *Republic* can be found primarily in Books II & III (377a -398b) and Book X 595a-608b. It is interesting to note a difference between these two accounts. In the first account Plato focuses on the specific pedagogical uses of art (primarily poetry) especially as they relate to the education of young people who will grow up to be citizens of the polis. In Book X the discussion is more theoretical and open-ended. Here Plato discusses and reaffirms why art as such must be looked at carefully and critically, but also concludes his discussion with an acknowledgment of the ancient and ongoing quarrel between art and philosophy including the admission (even if somewhat backhandedly) that the last words may not have been spoken on the matter (607b).

libertarians or communists within the "liberal-democratic" spectrum is an interesting theoretical question, but one that need not concern us in detail here. Both of these extreme endpoints are best viewed as unstable isotopes of the liberal-democratic form, and we will have reason to refer to them on occasion to help demonstrate or explain certain parts of our analysis. The middle of the liberal-democratic continuum consists of the manifold of liberal-democratic states and their accompanying ideologies that are distributed along this continuum, primarily according to their free-market versus socialist credentials. The more "free-market" a liberal democracy is the closer to the libertarian end of the continuum it is; while the more "socialist" a liberal-democracy is the nearer it comes to communism. I realize that this continuum is buffeted, crosscut and overlapped with other ideas and structures — sectarian, traditional, fundamentalist, fascistic. This manifold of cross and undercurrents can and often does dilute, compromise, and even sidetrack the liberal-democratic structures and ideas of any given political system or ideology. These impurities in the liberal-democratic alloy, though admittedly significant from a practical or historical point of view, are not pertinent to my argument. It is the liberal-democratic complex in its purer form that interests me because: 1) it encompasses what is considered these days, for good or bad, enlightened thought and practice on political matters; 2) it is the dominant (one might even say hegemonic) political form of our times; and 3) it constitutes the primary basis of our current common understanding of Plato's political philosophy.

I will now identify some commonalities that will be relevant to our inquiry and that make up the core of what I call the liberal-democratic complex. Some of these commonalities I have already hinted at in the previous two chapters; all will be discussed in greater detail as we proceed. Political ideologies that comprise the liberal-democratic complex are all children of the Enlightenment. This means at a minimum that for these ideologies, knowledge about political structures, practices and beliefs can only be based on scientific knowledge and/or logical reasoning. Knowledge claims that are based on traditional, transcendental and/or religious sources, for example, are strictly prohibited and inadmissible.[37] Different liberal-democratic ideologies of course do disagree about what in detail can be known about politics, that is, they disagree about what falls within the ambit of legitimate political knowledge. If we look at the endpoints of our liberal-democratic continuum, for example, we see that for the libertarian not much can be known about political matters, while for the communist the collection of things to know (scientifically) is much larger. Liberal democracies for this reason also differ on the kinds of political systems they seek to establish and defend — again, libertarians prefer a political system that is as small as it can possibly be, while communists (putatively) prefer a political system that is extremely robust if not all-inclusive.[38] Along with the limits on political knowledge that all liberal-democratic ideologies share — and in large measure because

---

37　Political orders that are founded upon ideologies within the liberal-democratic complex are for this reason normally referred to as "secular" or nonsectarian states, as opposed to traditional and/or religious ones.

38　Of course the difference between the libertarian and the communist is really just a matter of time. Like the libertarian (and ultimately for much the same reason) the communist looks forward to the withering away of the state. And once the communist ideal is achieved, one would be hard-pressed to define how the libertarian and communist differ except that they take a different route to get to the same place. Although we would like to say that liberal democracies avoid this anti-political bent of their more extreme brethren, it is hard to avoid the conclusion that really it's just a matter of inflection and again... time. There are two roads to the end of politics along the liberal-democratic continuum, and which road you take depends upon which way you are pointing. In the direction of libertarianism, the conservative free-market liberal democrat is always pushing and searching for ways to limit government and privatize its functions. In the direction of communism, the social democrat is always pushing and searching for ways to expand the role of "scientific" government so that ultimately the individual can be freed from the chains that prevent him/her from becoming the person they choose. In either case the inherent logic is emancipatory, and the object of this emancipation is the individual — an empty abstraction of pure potential who has been freed from the chains of politics.

of these very limitations — they also all adhere to some version of abstract individualism.[39] Abstract individualism is an idea in which individuals — when considered from the perspective of the political regime of which they are a part — have no preordained or prior content or characteristics that individuate them in any politically relevant way from anybody else. This is not the same as the concept of political equality *per se*, though it is easy to conflate the two notions. Political equality insofar as it exists does so usually as a goal and/or positive metric of actual liberal-democratic political orders. Abstract individualism alternatively is something that liberal-democratic ideologies posit as a brute parameter of the human condition that exists and persists regardless of time or place. Thus, the idea that "all men are created equal" is, under this interpretation, an expression of abstract individualism because it precedes the constitution of the political order and is meant to be true under all conditions — political or otherwise. We shall see in the analysis that follows that what makes all men equal in liberal-democratic eyes is their shared abstract individualism. Utopian communists and a host of fellow left-of-center travelers may insist that, quite unlike the standard bourgeois liberal view of the individual as empty abstraction, they look upon human beings in all their historical and communal richness. But that is true only in the sense that ideologies like Marxist-communism and its socialist companions tend

---

39    An apologist for liberalism like Kimlicka (1989) has argued that the idea of the abstract individual is not a necessary or even particularly coherent conclusion to be drawn from liberal principles. His adversaries in this argument are thinkers like Taylor (1992), MacIntyre (1981) and Sandal (1996). In my view Kimlicka's disagreements with the likes of a Taylor or a Sandal are internecine debates among members of what I have called the liberal-democratic complex. The fact of the matter is that Kimlicka and his adversaries are all looking for "community," and they all have a hard time getting their conceptual arms around this notion because they cannot identify a working notion of public life, and thus cannot talk about politics in a manner that does not ultimately break down into its private individualistic components — unless they make the move (not sanctioned by any form of liberal-democratic thinking) towards a transcendental cum non-natural source of social adhesive.

to stand free-market liberalism on its head. Just as the communist meets the libertarian once history comes to an end and the state withers away, the communist also posits the abstract individual as the end product of history — the new man of communism is the abstract individual who, by virtue of the material plenty that human history has ultimately created, gardens in the morning, hunts in the afternoon and writes poetry at night. Marx's much noted vagueness about what happens after "History comes to an end" is much the same as what we find in all liberal-democratic ideologies with their reliance on the abstract individual as an elemental political construct. The "what happens after the end of History" is, for Marx and liberal-democrat alike, ultimately what the abstract individual chooses to happen. As we will see below the abstract individual forms the basis of the liberal-democratic notion of freedom.

The pages that follow discuss and analyze Plato's notions on freedom, equality, political truth and art. What I have called liberal democracy or the liberal-democratic complex will play a prominent part in this discussion. The underlying assumption that I will try to explicate is that, from the Platonic perspective, the entire range of ideologies that I have huddled under the liberal-democratic umbrella all look quite similar and commit the same kinds of errors when it comes to understanding politics, the public realm and ultimately what it means for humans to live well. The reverse side of this similarity explains much about what I have previously identified in the two preceding chapters as the standard interpretation of Plato's political philosophy. In trying to revise or even overturn our received interpretations of Plato there is, then, the added goal of trying to revise or overturn the ways our own liberal-democratic ideologies have come to understand politics, the public realm and finally human well-being. The fact that these ideologies are strongly linked to the political systems of most of the developed nations in the contemporary world, and certainly the ones that drive our global economy forward, gives this project a measure of immediate significance.

## Freedom

Any concept of freedom is connected logically to two other complex areas of philosophical inquiry. One of these areas involves the very mechanics of human agency and tries to answer the question: What does it mean for humans to decide to do this rather than that? The other involves the content and extent of human knowledge, particularly as it pertains to the aforementioned capability for acting in this rather than that way. It seems that at a minimum the concept of freedom requires that we — at least in some significant number of instances — be able to choose our own course of action and that there be, further, some way to judge whether our choice was good or bad (right or wrong) according to some scale of value. From a practical point of view this last statement is easy to understand and in some measure totally non-controversial. It forms the basis as a matter of course for the way we look at many of our own actions and those of others, especially those actions we would consider ethically significant. Students of philosophy also know, however, that upon closer theoretical scrutiny the concept of freedom begins to unravel in both directions — that of human agency as well as that of human knowledge.

Let's start with agency. The concept of agency becomes problematic once we begin to look for the causes of our actions as well as the object or the organ whereupon these causes do their work. These two components are bound tightly together because it is presumed that in order for freedom to be a genuine characteristic of human activity, both the cause and what the cause is affecting must be virtually (if not literally) one and the same thing. The concept of "free will" has, in western civilization, tried to capture this requirement that "free" human acts be self-initiated or self-caused. Unfortunately once western philosophers and scientists started to "drill down" into concepts like the "will" or the "self," they found that they are more like convenient abstractions used to identify complexes of brain-body transactions than anything tangible or resolutely identifiable as the seat and source of human action. Explanations about why humans do what they do or what within the human animal performs these actions have not found anything like a will or self that can rightly be called the seat of free agency. Even if we grant that the experience of our own agency (that I seem to decide to do this rather than that) must point to some kind of actual process (or set of processes), it remains difficult to describe and understand what it is about this process that is properly called "free" or "me" — in any rigorous or inter-subjectively identifiable sense.

We can step back a bit and observe that there are indeed what appear to be the obvious counter-factual cases in which external factors constrain us from doing what we would otherwise (and freely) choose to do. According to our common sense logic, if those outside factors are removed, we then become free to do as we please. The problem on closer analysis, however, is again drawing the line between what is external versus what is internal — external and internal to what?[40] We want to answer to "us"... but what specifically constitutes this "us" part? The "us" that inhabits our bodies and provides the locus and content of our putatively free actions seems more like a ghost in a machine than anything that either science or philosophy can identify and treat as the seat and cause of our putatively freely chosen actions. All actions instead appear to follow from chains of cause and effect that do not point to anything like a freely choosing agent. Rather they seem to indicate that we are machines, albeit of an incredibly complex biological sort, which are determined and acted upon by forces and laws of nature. And, in this way, we are no different than anything else in the universe.

---

40    And as Daniel Dennett whimsically observes, this line of argument can be reduced to absurdity: "If you make yourself really small, you can externalize everything." Daniel Dennett (2003) pp. 122-126.

The conclusions thinkers have drawn from what begins to re-semble the futile search for the mechanisms and the locus of free-dom, have depended on the thinker (and more often then not, his/her political and moral agenda). Some have brashly accepted that free human agency, as conventionally understood, is indeed an il-lusion which hides the more fundamental processes of our body that along with the forces and factors of an impinging environment actually do determine how we think and act. Others have re-in-terpreted the idea of freedom so that it fits within the brain-body machine complex that defines and houses our agency. Freedom in this guise is the experience we have of this agency. This experience consists primarily of a variety of forms of information processing that over time builds and modifies that thing we come to call our self (that is, the "us"). This repositioning of the idea of freedom has resembled more an attempt to argue that freedom (not to say will) is simply the wrong word to use when talking about human activity. Whether you accept that freedom is simply an illusion or you try to reposition and redefine these terms, the issue doggedly always boils down to how a theoretical understanding of human action, as essentially a function of ongoing physical forces, factors and processes, can be related to the thoughts and practices we have of each other as human agents who deploy and utilize ideas and ex-periences such as freedom, will and the self. Under views of either sort — the rejection of freedom or its repositioning — it is hard not to reach the conclusion that human agency, as we normally under-stand it, is an illusion and that what "we" really experience is at best a kind of theatre or phenomenal representation of the things going on in the biological machine that we are. Of course, what conclu-sions the human machine in turn reaches, and what actions follow from these conclusions, are themselves entirely a function of how the machine works while it interacts with itself and its environ-ment. Viewed in this light, our experience of agency and our pecu-liar way of talking about it — by employing terms like freedom and self — constitute one facet among many (and not even necessarily a very important one) of the way the human machine has evolved.[41] Still, there remains at least the uncomfortable sense that if all this were substantially true — and we knew and acknowledged it to be true — we would be hard-pressed to conduct our lives and look upon our fellow humans in the ways that we find both familiar and warranted. One suspects that our moral and political ideas and practices would have to undergo a significant revision if not complete transmutation.[42]

There are then, not surprisingly, still others who go beyond nature and the brain-body machine and have posited the existence of some kind of transcendental entity that is the substance and source of our individual human freedom. This kind of position exits the realm of science and philosophy and enters that of religion and theology. The inherent weakness of moral and political positions that are not based on reason and logic, but rather on things like faith and revelation, is that they ultimately require conversion and adherence to beliefs that are profoundly (not to say literally) unreasonable. The danger (and it is one that has been played out in human history time and again) is that when moral and political disagreements and impasses of a fundamental sort are reached between people who hold beliefs of this kind, there are few if any mechanisms for adjudicating them short of the use of force.

---

41   One could explain concepts like freedom, will and self as adaptations to human consciousness, which in turn could be described as an offshoot or spandrel of the creation of higher brain functions. The evolution of larger more intelligent brains may result in the creation of that space in our head we call self-consciousness. That space however, in and of itself, may not do anything other than let the brain do what it has to do, for example, it gives the human machine a mechanism for handling the idea of death (which is itself a by-product of our higher intelligence). Ultimately we may also surmise that someday the humans may evolve into animals that have found a way to achieve higher intelligence without all the inconveniences of (self) consciousness and the ineffable apparatus of free human agency.

42   This is Berlin's point that he makes repeatedly in his essay "Historical Inevitability" (1969) pp. 41-117.

One begins to suspect that perhaps Plato's reticence on the con-cept of freedom was less a deficiency of his thinking and more an enlightened appreciation for the stubborn intractability (perhaps even absurdity) of the concept itself. Still, modern political opinion remains wedded to the notion that unencumbered human activity — free action — is a value worth pursuing. The major reason this remains true, despite our inability to find and define the seat of our free human agency, involves the other side of the freedom equation — human knowledge. It is here that we begin to appreciate why Plato's silences about freedom seem inappropriate to the modern ear. At the same time, I will begin to investigate why this silence may speak about some truths once told but now forgotten.

The relationship of knowledge to the concept of freedom can be broken down roughly into two categories. The first, and easier of the two, includes knowledge that is of an instrumental sort. This kind of knowledge helps us do the things we want to do by informing us primarily about how to do them. The other category of knowledge is the kind that helps us to decide or even helps "determine" what we want to do. This kind of knowledge can be called moral or po-litical knowledge if the decisions it helps us take include actions and consequences that impact in a significant (as opposed to triv-ial) way on the lives and well-being of ourselves and other people. As a conventional description of knowledge and how it relates to the idea of freedom it is, like our initial description of free agency itself, easy to understand because it makes distinctions that, from a practical point of view, make a kind of self-evident sense.

Once again, it is when philosophy turns its theoretical gaze onto the subject of knowledge itself that questions and problems arise. The validity of all forms of human knowing can and has been put into question by a variety of philosophical schools and has, in turn, been salvaged and defended by an equal variety of said schools, some of them assuming the role of both critic and defender. The complicated arc of the history of epistemology within just our western philosophical tradition is a difficult subject to encompass, and I make no pretense to do so here. Nevertheless, the current state of affairs can be epitomized with some accuracy and certainly enough for the purposes of this discussion.

Of the two categories of knowledge that tend to be applicable to (free) human action, instrumental knowledge has fared far better than moral-political knowledge. At its core, instrumental knowledge is closely linked to the forms and methods of modern science. The forms and methods of modern science are by no means monolithic or non-controversial from a philosophical *cum* epistemological point of view. Nevertheless, instrumental knowledge and the science that backs it up have been invariably able to trump most of their putative theoretical shortcomings by virtue of their very instrumentality. It may be the case that things like formal logic or particle physics are expressions of a male-dominated political power structure (and not as pure, pristine and objective as scientists claim), but no one can deny the practical efficacy that follows from employing these kinds of "knowledge" to send rockets to the moon or create unearthly sources of energy. No such trump card comes into play once we turn our attentions from instrumental to moral and political knowledge. In this case, quite to the contrary, the very idea that such knowledge actually exists has been thrown into question. Indeed, the dominant western political ideologies that form the liberal-democratic complex (and its steadfast companion, free-market capitalism) are founded on the very notion that substantive moral and political knowledge are, in large measure, unattainable.

It is at this point in our inquiry where we can begin to glimpse how Plato's political philosophy achieved its fairly nasty reputation overall, including its neglect or silence on the concept of freedom. Plato clearly claimed and argued that moral and political knowledge is in some degree and in some manner achievable. He also appeared to claim further that this knowledge is of the kind that can tell us what actions are good and bad, right and wrong; and it is precisely this latter claim that we moderns tend to find most troublesome. It is moreover this claim that also makes it easy for us to understand why Plato's philosophy did not seem to mention or place any emphasis on something that we would recognize as the notion of freedom. There is a linkage in Plato's philosophy between knowledge and action that is tightly drawn. Sometimes it looks like Plato claimed that knowing what is right is tantamount to doing what is right. His philosophy does not appear to allow for any mechanism that would explain how a human could choose to do something bad if said human knows what is good. The connection between knowledge and action in Plato appears to operate more like logical entailment than "free choice." Just as one does not choose whether 1 + 1 will equal 2, one ostensibly cannot choose to do what is right if you know what is right... one does it, nearly or virtually by definition. Of course, as I have tried to argue, many of the concerns and criticisms we have with Plato tend to treat aspects of his thought, such as the structure of knowledge and the structure of the world, in a way that makes these concerns and criticisms both understandable and fair. Before we examine more closely how this affects the way we think about Plato's position on the matter of freedom, let us return briefly to how the ideologies that form the liberal-democratic complex treat the notion of moral and political knowledge.

The claim that liberal democracy in all its many forms is founded on the idea that moral and political knowledge is not available would certainly strike many of us as peculiar if not dead wrong. After all, don't the many forms of liberal-democratic governments that we know of have a great deal to say about what constitutes a political order, and what rights we humans have in relation to that order? Don't these democracies claim to know and have a great deal to say about a whole array of moral and political matters by virtue of the laws they make and the judgments they render? Yes, that is true, with this caveat: A liberal-democratic ideology in its purest form does not allow, and in fact prohibits, the generation of knowledge and judgments about any substantive moral and political issue that are derived from the liberal-democratic ideology itself. Liberal-democracies as liberal-democracies are purposely silent about what human actions are good or bad, just or unjust. Instead and in lieu of this knowledge (and the judgments it would inform), liberal-democratic political systems are set up to provide each of their individual citizens with as much "freedom" to pursue and express their own ideas and practices concerning what is good, right and just. Any kind of liberal democracy in its pristine form, then, is (and only is) "a framework for freedom." This framework has both "public" and "private" facets in that individuals or collections of individuals "pursue their happiness," and thus exercise their freedom either through the structures of the political system itself, or within structures of a private realm that exists beyond the positive reach of the political system, yet whose integrity and security are policed and maintained by that system. Not surprisingly then, one of the inherent tensions within liberal-democratic ideologies is the collective or majority expressions of what is good, right and just versus individual or minority positions on the same matters that diverge and are in conflict with them. The former become especially problematic when they are implemented, sanctioned and/or administered by the legitimate power structures of the political order itself. Arguments for individual and/or minority rights within liberal-democratic theory find their most compelling rationale as the last and ineliminable line of defense against collective and/or majority "abuses" of power. A fundamental problem with liberal-democratic thought and practice is that all uses of political power that are not, strictly speaking, procedural in nature are *prima facie* abuses of power. The only legitimate uses of power that a liberal democracy can engage in or sanction, *qua* liberal democracy, are those that implement and administer the framework within which individuals pursue their own individual or group ends. Any laws or political acts that go beyond the building and maintenance of the "framework of freedom" are illegitimate by definition. Of course, a great deal of political argument and action has been spent trying to define and establish what exactly constitutes building and maintaining this framework, including how to recognize uses of power that go beyond their procedural and custodial charges. Popular political arguments, for example, between the left and right, or between social democrats and free-market conservatives, are essentially about where to draw the line between legitimate and illegitimate uses of what is always in the final analysis "procedural" political power.

It should be noted that what I have just now called the liberal-democratic "framework of freedom" denotes a particularly empty notion of freedom, and that this emptiness is a direct result of the liberal-democratic position that moral and political knowledge is either publicly unattainable and/or simply nonexistent. Moral and political knowledge (or belief) — insofar as it exists for the liberal democrat at all — is the private preserve of each and every individual citizen. The pursuit and expression of this individually acquired "knowledge" constitutes in turn the highest good of any liberal-democratic ideology.

The careful reader may want to point out that individuals who pursue their own happiness within what I have called the liberal-democratic "framework of freedom" are actually prohibited from acquiring and using political knowledge of any sort other than the specific knowledge that justifies and installs the liberal-democratic framework itself. Therefore, the kinds of knowledge (or beliefs) that citizens of liberal democracies are actually authorized to pursue, hold and/or employ, are more aptly described as private and moral and not genuinely public or political at all. Our understanding and evaluation of this private-public distinction is particularly germane to understanding our prevailing interpretations and valuations of Plato's political philosophy, including his purported lack of interest in freedom.

It is obvious enough that the world Plato lived in and wrote about and the world that we now live in differ in many respects. Some of these differences are very significant and pertinent to any discussion of moral and political philosophy. The underlying presumption as we continue to study the thought of someone like Plato, is that despite whatever differences in historical context arise, there remains something about the human condition, a commonality, which allows humans to speak to each other over what are sometimes vast reaches of time and place. The danger in looking for commonalities of this sort is that it frequently involves abstracting putative kernels of theoretical truth from the rich density of a practical historical context. We encountered the effects of this kind of process above in our discussion of the Cave myth, specifically, where we saw how the historical relationship between Socrates and his actual political adversaries, the Sophists, tended to be distilled from interpretations of Plato's arguments and positions. When we start to examine notions such as private and public and how these ideas (and the constellation of institutions and practices that embody them) might differ between Plato and us, and further, how this difference may explain our differing views on freedom, the issue becomes even more complex. Let's start with Plato.

The concepts of public and private for Plato are tightly linked if not identical to another pair of concepts — politics and economics, respectively. The adjective "public" applies to actions or events that occur among and before a group of people that collectively constitutes a political order (in ancient Greece, invariably a *polis* or city). The adjective "private" applies to actions and events that occur away from and beyond this same group of collectively organized people. The paradigmatic location for these "private activities" is the household. In Plato's time, the house was the locus for private activity and especially the kinds of activities that sustained the livelihood of its members (not surprisingly then, the word "economics" finds its etymological roots in the Greek word for household).[43] The configuration of Greek politics and the private households that sustained the individuals who engaged in public action was largely exclusionary by our enlightened standards. The normal Greek *polis* included as genuine citizens primarily landholding men of a certain age, not to say pedigree (since to hold land meant to have some kind of pedigree). Excluded from the public realm were all the women, children, slaves and assorted aliens/artisans who, though they lived within the very bounds of the political order did not, by virtue of what they were, have a full-fledged public status. Activity and membership in the public realm were thus restricted to a minority of individuals who were part of a much larger whole that was made up of the private households that fell within the legal and geographical boundaries of the political order. Making and maintaining these legal and political boundaries (positive fictions nonetheless) was the primary activity of citizenship; and, engaging in civic activity was for Plato and his fellow Greeks the necessary foundation of human goodness, virtue and happiness.

To the modern ear the story of Plato's Greece is a familiar one, and also one that we fairly effortlessly conjugate within a movement of progressive enlightenment that has ushered into our own ideas and beliefs about the value and validity of modern liberal democracies. According to this story, the restrictive and exclusive political orders that populated the ancient Greek world have since become the open and inclusive liberal democracies of our time. Western political thought and belief (at the least) holds this achievement to be something of a crowning jewel, even to the point of identifying it as the end of the process. Under the umbrella of this self-congratulatory conjugation, the minority citizen-men of ancient Greece have been joined by their fellow humans — women, slaves, craftsmen

---

43  There is of course a long and complicated history of how economic activity has come to reside within a broad range of structures from the household to the multinational corporation. Certainly part of that history explains how what was once public activity became devalued or redefined within the ever expanding scope of economic power and activity.

and even children (as citizens *in vitro*, so to speak) — in an emanci-patory opening up of public space and political action. Moreover, it is precisely this freedom — to be a participant in politics — which the standard interpretation of Plato has wheeled into place when it accuses him of either missing the notion of freedom entirely or posi-tively thinking against it. It is also clear that even though Plato's depiction of the ideal political order in *Republic* is not exclusionary or restrictive in the same manner as was the Greek *polis* of his time, it still leaves the vast majority of people who inhabit his *polis* (spe-cifically, the workers) outside the ambit of genuine political and public thought and action. Most of the people who live in Plato's *Republic* are private members of households who are the stewards of the ruling (and publicly active) political class.

Plato's aristocracy of philosophers and guardians are an exclu-sive set of political agents who have been selected and educated according to a strict regimen that makes them what they are: the architects, administrators and guardians of a good and just politi-cal order. The lynchpin of Plato's *Republic* is knowledge of the good. Packed within this lynchpin are the claims that a) the good exists; b) it can be known; and c) that once known it can be implemented and institutionalized in some manner.[44] All three of these claims are in some (very strong) measure denied by all versions of liberal-democratic thought, and it is this denial that forms the basis of the conception of freedom that we are most inclined to value and de-fend against a political philosophy such as Plato's. According to the liberal-democratic creed there is no such thing as "the good" that can be known let alone put into practice; it is in lieu of this that

---

44   We will discuss in chapter four what it means to implement and in-stitutionalize Plato's ideas. From the outset, however, we must emphasize and reemphasize that Plato's political philosophy, especially as seen in his *Republic*, is not a blueprint for making just political systems. It is a tool... but a tool of a special sort.

each individual is "free" to define and realize his or her own private conception of the "good."[45]

It is important to highlight a point that I have previously made, namely that the issues of free agency and moral knowledge — deemed integral to a working theoretical conception of human freedom from a philosophical perspective — are within all forms of liberal-democratic ideology completely skirted. The denial of "the good," coupled with the notion that freedom consists primarily in finding one's "own good," form the basis of the standard modern criticisms of Plato as an opponent of freedom. This opposition to Plato leaves totally unexamined (not to say unsubstantiated) the seat of agency, as well as the standards by which our ideas and actions will be judged, except in the aforementioned sense that those ideas and actions which endanger or disrupt the framework of freedom itself are prohibited.

The kinds of criticisms of Plato's notion of freedom that we have examined are common fare and most readers are apt to agree with them at least on some level. The problems with this, as I see it, are twofold: First, as I have already argued, the conventional interpretations of Plato's political philosophy are fundamentally shortsighted. Yes, it is correct that Plato argued that there is such a thing as the good, that this good could be known, and that once known, it could be implemented and institutionalized within a just political order — *in some way*. But these arguments, especially as they are presented in *Republic*, are invariably couched within a rich irony and ambiguity, including and most tellingly so, in the myth of the Cave. This irony and ambiguity are most emphatically not incidental to Plato's philosophy. In other words they are not merely artistic, idiosyncratic or historical artifacts. They are, rather, central to understanding it. Second, correcting the prevailing shortcomings and misunderstandings that we may have concerning Plato's political philosophy is not primarily about getting the historical record right.

---

45   This is sometimes referred to in liberal-democratic parlance as "flourishing" — a particularly apt expression because it is an empty one.

Nor is it about trying to offer up an alternative political outlook and recipe like a return, let us say, to the Golden Age of Athens. What is important about gaining a better understanding of Plato's political ideas is that in doing so we also gain a more incisive perspective of our own moral and political environment. I admit this sounds rather trite, even fatuous, and it would be if all I meant was that the close study of the moral and political philosophy of a serious thinker like Plato gives us better self-understanding. What I mean instead is that Plato's philosophy provides what I believe is a singularly illuminating counterpoint to our prevailing moral and political thoughts and practices, as they are expressed and acted upon under the umbrella of an overarching liberal-democratic ideology.[46] This will hopefully become apparent as we conclude our examination of Plato and the concept of freedom, and it will become even more so as we move on to the other topics of equality, noble lying and art, and finally to chapter four where we will examine more fully the implications of a reinterpretation of Plato's political philosophy.

One of the reasons that criticisms of Plato on the subject of freedom have purchase is his avowed distaste for "democracy" as a political form. The concepts of democracy and freedom are inherently linked in liberal democracies quite obviously because democracy is theoretically the most inclusive — which is to say, freedom-giving — form of political organization. Thus any movement away from the ideal of all-inclusiveness and towards any form of exclusivity is

---

46  Most readers, I suspect, continue to wince at what may appear to them as a gross oversimplification of our contemporary political landscape. Let me reiterate and reemphasize that at a certain fundamental level — and precisely the level at which I am pitching my argument — contemporary western political ideologies share certain notions about things that make them, especially from the perspective of Plato's thought, the same. Thus, along the broad political spectrum that includes libertarians on one end and communists on the other, there is a commonality that I have — for lack of a better term — called the liberal-democratic complex. This spectrum does exclude atavistic and fundamentalist kinds of political thought and action, because they are fundamentally non-rational if not irrational. I would consider fascism and all forms of theocracy, for example, to fall into other (non-liberal democratic) ideological buckets.

*prima facie* a restraint on freedom — an obstacle to the pursuit and realization of our own individual notion of happiness and good-ness.[47] Most critics of Plato would accuse him of having denied this ideal of "free" self-determination — including not endorsing the democratic order it implicitly if not explicitly requires — and in turn of supporting the authoritative pronouncements and assigna-tions of a knowing and knowledgeable philosopher-king and his guardian lieutenants. For Plato, the great run of people within a city cannot possibly be left to their own political devices when it comes to determining what is good and just and ultimately what will make for their "happiness." In some blank unimaginative sense this is all too true. Guilty as charged.

Still, the dividing line along which enlightened liberal democrats differ from the ancient (pre-enlightened) Plato is not so easily de-scribed, not to say understood. Our celebration of freedom is, ac-cording to Plato's way of thinking, a capitulation to ignorance; it is more akin to neglect or even irresponsibility than a grant of some universally desired and readily implemented political rite of pas-sage — "free at last." And, it is more than simply an assertion that liberal democracies fail to prepare their citizens for freedom; for in-deed, there are many variations of liberal-democratic thought and practice which argue that it is the obligation of the political order (a duty of the framework of freedom) to educate and prepare its citizens for the freedom they will enjoy, that is, to give them the tools as well as the opportunity to be free. The fundamental prob-lem for Plato is that this grant of freedom is literally misplaced; it occurs in a location that cannot deliver on its promises. Modern freedom is something that happens in "the home," or to speak in the modern idiom, within the economic sphere; for this reason it

---

47    As previously noted, the only kinds of exclusions that are warrant-ed under liberal democracies are those that are required to establish and maintain the framework of freedom within which our freedom to pursue our own individual ends takes place. What exclusions are so warranted, of course, is subject to considerable dispute.

is fundamentally a private affair. To the extent that all these private expressions and realizations of freedom have a public or communitarian face they are best described as an aggregate expression or collection of individual private freedoms. From the extreme libertarian to the staunch communist and all the liberal-democratic variants in between, there is essentially no end use for politics as politics. Its value is completely instrumental and, under extreme utopian formulas, ultimately expendable. If there are such things as the good, justice and happiness for liberal-democratic ideologies, these values are empty of any inherent political content and cannot be expressed let alone realized as public goods. Given this, it is not hard to appreciate that a thinker such as Plato, whose own notions of the good, justice and happiness are based on robust notions of of politics and public life, would strike the modern ear as seriously out of tune. Yet, it needs to be noted finally that there is in reality no point of contention between Plato and liberal-democratic theory over the concept of freedom at all. The real point of difference between contemporary liberal-democratic thought and practice and Plato's political philosophy is their widely different conception of politics and the public realm. For liberal democrats, politics and the public realm at their very best harbor and expedite our pursuit of happiness, and at their worst get in its way; whereas for Plato, politics and the public realm constitute and indeed contain whatever happiness we can hope to achieve as human beings.

From Plato's perspective the conceptions of politics and the public realm that one finds within all liberal democracies are radically devalued and foreshortened. The issue is further compounded, in his view, by the close connection between freedom and democracy that exists in liberal-democratic theory and practice. Plato's aforementioned "distaste" for democracy can now be unpacked and understood. There are two components to this. First, in a democracy no distinction can be drawn between private interests and the public good because there are no political agents that are assigned to champion or stand for the latter against the former. Public officials are all chosen from and represent the interests of the private households from which they are chosen. This (not incidentally) is entirely what informs the problem Aristotle had in rounding out his topology of good and bad forms of government.[48] Whereas according to Aristotle a king represents the common good of his kingdom, a tyrant treats his kingdom as if it were his own household. Whereas an aristocracy represents the common good of the *polis*, an oligarchy treats the *polis* as if it were its own collection of households. A democracy cannot be theoretically identified as good or bad in these terms because it represents itself — the entire collection of private households. Politics in a democracy becomes a competition over whose interests will become identified with and implemented by the political system — a not unfamiliar description of things.

Secondly, a democracy holds to the notion that there are no inherent requirements needed to engage in political thought and action. The only requirement is citizenship and in a democracy everyone is a citizen, or if not a citizen, then a potential one. Although most liberal-democratic political systems erect barriers to citizenship and even add to these when it comes to the requirements for holding public office, such barriers are essentially *ad hoc* and based on prudential rather than strictly theoretical *a priori* considerations. The absence of any inherent qualifications to hold public office is

---

48  Aristotle's topology of good and bad political orders is undoubtedly based on Plato's own topology which he introduces in *Republic* at the end of Book IV but does not complete, several digressions later, until Book IX. Plato's version aligns fives kinds of orders from best to worst: Kingship, Aristocracy, Democracy, Oligarchy and Tyranny. Democracy is not the worse form of *polis* in this taxonomy though it is, as described by Plato, the first step towards true political disorder. As such it represents the initial disappearance of public interests and the ascendance of private ones, culminating ultimately in tyranny where all interests of the polis are located in the private person of the tyrant. Aristotle's re-configuration of this typology is certainly related to his criticisms of Plato's political philosophy. Having rejected the metaphysical and epistemological underpinnings of Plato's typology (namely the good and the knowledge of same) he cannot arrange his topology in the descending normative order that Plato uses.

directly related to the limitations that liberal democracies place on political knowledge, coupled with the idea of the abstract individual. Once again the extreme ends of the liberal-democratic continuum prove this rule by virtue of what appears to be their exception to it. Accordingly, neither libertarians nor communists ultimately leave any room whatsoever for political thought and action as such. Whatever remains of the political order and its functions become in each case a matter of technical expertise — what is described as the mere administration of things. Though this may seem to contradict the notion that there are no requirements to hold public office, by substituting for it the idea that public officials should have technical expertise, the contradiction is more apparent than real. Indeed, the technical expert is actually a figure that pervades the entire spectrum of ideologies within the liberal-democratic complex and is not unique to either the libertarian or the communist extremes. Rather, there is among all free-market and socialist variations of liberal-democratic ideologies the belief that many (if not all) of the things that a government legitimately does can ultimately be implemented by experts in the fields of knowledge pertinent to what it is that the government is supposed to do. The idea of civil servants whose qualifications are based on objectively established standards of merit is never far from any liberal-democratic political order.

At first glance, and surprisingly so, it may appear that this idea comes straight out of Plato and in some measure it does. In form it clearly resembles Plato; the difference is in its content. Civil servants, as conceived by liberal democracies, are civil servants not because they have knowledge of politics and the public sphere, but precisely because they have expert knowledge that makes what they do neither political nor essentially public. The idea of the expert civil servant resembles in form Plato's own position that the rulers of a political order should have knowledge specific to what it is they are doing. The difference is that for Plato, this knowledge does not trump politics and the public sphere but is actually and necessarily about both of them. Plato's "expert" rulers are political and public figures precisely because the knowledge they have extends into the very realm prohibited by liberal-democratic ideologies — namely the individual and his collective existence. We shall see this in greater detail and from a different angle as we now move to our analysis of equality.

## Equality

We discussed briefly the idea of equality as it pertains to the liberal-democratic notion of freedom, and in many respects it is this pertinence that forms the core of our current thoughts about human equality. Before we move on to any discussion of equality in its own right, we should make note that there is an obvious and generally accepted sense in which human beings are not equal, not at all. There is a wide and palpable array of categories — physical appearance and intelligence to mention two obvious ones — along which human beings differ quite markedly one from the other. Whatever it is that any thinker or ideological outlook may mean by the word equality as it applies to human beings, we can safely assume that they are not talking about a strict or broad identity between individual people. It would seem, then, that if the concept of equality is to be successfully applied to human beings, it must identify or refer to some element(s) or aspect(s) of our humanity that we all have in common to some equivalent degree. At first blush there does not seem to be much to quarrel with here. After all, if humans can be successfully identified as humans there must arguably be something common about our humanity on which we can hang the concept of equality. As our analysis moves forward we will see that the liberal-democratic notion of equality does adhere to a notion like this, namely, that it is our common humanity that defines our equality; although we will also see that this notion is not as straightforward as it might seem. My reason for engaging in what may appear a rather facile discussion about the obvious differences between individual people and the things that we as humans puta-tively have in common, is that it is precisely this transition — from the obvious differences between individuals to some attribution of generic equality — that constitutes the important difference be-tween Plato's thoughts on political equality and that of all modern liberal-democratic ideologies (including the libertarian and com-munist isotopes). As our discussion proceeds we will begin to see why this so.

We had reason to observe in our previous discussion on freedom that there are two concepts of "equality" that circulate in liberal-democratic ideologies. One is the brute "fact" of equality that is part of the foundation of liberal-democratic political orders, and undoubtedly best captured in the liberal-democratic mantra that all men (and now women) are created equal. It is this brute self-evident parameter, moreover, that is more easily identified with the argument that there is something, *qua* human, that all humans share and that forms the basis of their equality, including and especially their "political" equality. The other concept of equality that we iden-tified refers to the positive laws, structures and actions enacted and undertaken by political orders as a means to implement and admin-ister some measure of equality among individuals, and is exempli-fied in such commonplaces of liberal democracies as equality before the law and equal opportunity. These two uses of the concept of equality — one brute and one more accurately portrayed as positive or legal — are obviously different yet also obviously related in some manner, especially as they are understood by a liberal-democratic sensibility. It is this relationship that we will examine next.

The brute equality that plays a founding part in modern liberal-democratic theory and ultimately informs the practice of modern liberal-democratic governments would appear to be, by virtue of its very self-evident nature, difficult to articulate beyond the ex-planation that in some measure, and along some species index or set of registers, humans are equal. The extent to which humans are equal and the actual content of this equality is, not surprisingly, subject to dispute. Indeed, it can be argued that it is its very disputability, or rather its complete lack of definite specificity, that best describes the nature of this brute equality — the adjective being particularly apt since it is an equality that is roundly inarticulate. Yet, even this is not exactly correct. A more precise definition of fundamental equality as it functions in liberal-democratic theory and practice might be stated more accurately this way: Because of the limits of human knowledge there is no actual way to determine specifically in what way and to what degree individual people are and are not equal, so it is best to act "as if" all individuals are in fact equal in some significant sense.[49] This default and essentially empty assignation of equality is yet another aspect of the liberal-democratic way of conceiving of human beings as abstract individuals who are — at least when looked at from the theoretical perspective — basically empty vessels of material and moral potentiality. As was the case with freedom — where each individual is free (within some set of formal limits that are set by the political order) to define the purposes and pleasures of his or her individual life — all liberal-democratic citizens are equal by virtue of their abstract emptiness. In its most sanguine formulation, individuals are equal precisely because they can become (again from the perspective of the political order) whatever they choose to become. This brute equality of liberal-democratic thought and action actually forms the theoretical baseline from which each individual begins his or her ostensibly free project of self-definition, their individual pursuit of happiness.

It is from this empty baseline of equality that the positive laws, practices and structures of political equality stem in liberal democracies. The primary purpose of these positive elements is not, how-

---

49   A variety of liberal political theorists (starting most notably with Thomas Hobbes) have employed what have become known as arguments from an original position. This kind of argument almost always tries to establish human equality on the basis of the limits of human knowledge in some form. Undoubtedly the most renowned is that of John Rawls. See (1971).

ever, to define what political or legal equality consists in but, quite to the contrary, to insure that no such definite determinations are made. The mechanisms of positive political equality in liberal democracies act somewhat counterintuitively as the primary enablers of individual differentiation. We see then more specifically what the relationship is between equality and freedom as it is conceived by the typical liberal democrat. The equality of the individual is an empty abstraction that is off-limits to the political order. A liberal-democratic political order cannot legitimately delineate what is, so to speak, inside an individual, and by implication it cannot seek to develop or modify said individual in any particular predetermined way. This "hands-off" approach on the part of the political order is considered to be one of the primary merits of liberal democracy and, in turn (and not surprisingly), is considered to be a major problem with Plato's political thought.

Universal public education offers an illuminating if not central example of how political equality works in liberal-democratic political systems, but also illustrates some of the tensions and problems that accompany it. The core concept behind the idea of universal public education is that the political order should try to provide each of its young subjects with a basic set of skills and minimum cache of knowledge that will enable them to become healthy and productive citizens. As the child grows and develops to adulthood, he/she will begin to guide their own education into the more specific skills and areas of their choosing. The process, in theory, treats each child equally. In the simplifying language of liberal-democratic political ideology, each child can work to become whatever he/she wants — policeman, doctor, homemaker... nuclear physicist. We can express this in terms of our present analysis as: Each child is initially equal to become under the benign aegis of the liberal-democratic "framework of freedom" whatever he/she chooses. Of course, sophisticated advocates and defenders of the idea of universal public education are likely to react with a collective grimace at so stark and simplistic a characterization of what liberal-democratic orders are up to when they legislate, implement and administer policies of public education.[50] Moreover, there are admittedly a wide variety of ways in which the idea of universal public education is articulated and realized by the many different versions of liberal democracy past and present. The differences among the numerous historical and contemporary examples of public education in liberal democracies are, for my immediate purposes, not important. As for the stark simplicity of my characterization let me now proceed to demonstrate that, though it is surely stark and simple, it nevertheless captures accurately the fault line between Plato's ideas about equality and our own liberal-democratic ones.

An obvious shortcoming of universal public education is that although "students" may be given the equal (which is to say unencumbered) opportunity to become whatever it is they want to become, they often fail. There are many forms this "failure" can take, though most can be characterized as either a failure to properly identify one's career path or, having chosen the right path, a failure to work hard enough to achieve success along that path. Young people fail to become the happy adults they assuredly want to become because they don't know what they want; or, when they do know, they don't try hard enough to get it. In all cases it is ultimately the individual who fails and not the institutions of public education that are there to help them on their way. Granted, institutions of public education (and indeed a whole host of public and private institutions) are not so easily exonerated in practice because they can be criticized for failing to provide the right guidance, the right tools or even the right encouragement to insure that students will become what they want to become. This is true enough, and arguments abound and

---

50  One needs to be cautious sometimes with "sophisticated" positions because they can be used to hide the obvious behind a flurry of (sometimes impenetrable) complexity. In this instance the look back to sophistic arguments that Socrates works to simplify (and thereby clarify) is completely intended.

proliferate over what constitutes the right guidance, the correct set of tools and the necessary amounts of encouragement to insure success. At the same time all these arguments about the means towards the ends of universal public education tend to hide its theoretical underpinnings — its ur-assumption about the individual — and these clearly place the final burden of equality and the grant of freedom fully in the hands of the individual. One is inclined to conclude — especially if one is a good liberal democrat — that, ideally, this is as it should be. And I would agree — but let us be certain about what we agree about.

We may be tempted to bring the argument to an end at this point and to summarily declare that the differences between our own liberal-democratic ideas on equality and those of Plato are primarily a function of how much knowledge and power a political order will have over its citizens in determining what it is they will become within the overarching social order — butcher, baker, soldier, sailor, so to speak. We can observe accordingly that liberal democracies take a "hands-off" approach to public education while Plato's approach as detailed in *Republic* is extremely "hands-on" — indeed we are inclined to say that his methods are excessively intrusive. Moreover this difference in methodology is one that applies not only to public education, but also to the manner in which political knowledge and power are conceived and applied throughout the entire social order. We meet once again the conventional wisdom about Plato and how his political thought compares to our own political ideologies and systems. Once more we confront the meddlesome, authoritarian Plato who compares badly with our own enlightened, tolerant and empowering ideas and policies. However, and as was the case with our examination of the idea of freedom, there is a hidden operator in this argument that tends to distort how we look at Plato's thought as well as misleads us when we look at our own political thoughts and actions.

We can see this hidden operator if we return to our previous discussion about how the terms political-public and economic-private are understood and employed by Plato versus how they tend to be understood and deployed by modern liberal-democratic thinkers. You will recall that for a classical Greek like Plato, the political and the public were tightly woven together as were the economic and the private. Each pair of concepts refers to a distinct set of ideas and practices that cut across and delineate virtually the entire social order, separating them into the economic sphere of the "household" and political sphere of public governance. Along the ancient Greek register of human valuation it was the latter political realm that directed and protected the former private, economic one. And it was in this capacity of governor and guardian of the private economic realm that the political realm of public administration achieved its status as the "highest" form of human activity. Within the liberal-democratic complex we can observe how these two distinct pairings become unraveled and completely revaluated. At the top of the liberal-democratic value register stands the abstract individual whose meaning and purpose in life is developed and defined by activity within what is, from the ancient Greek vantage point, the private economic sphere. Politics shows up on the value register more as a subset of economics and acts, at best, as an enabler and protector of the structures and processes of private self-realization (the framework of freedom). A career in politics within the liberal-democratic scheme is just that — a career choice from among the many career choices available to each individual. In this way politics becomes thoroughly subsumed and ultimately absorbed by economics. We saw above in our discussion on freedom that prevailing conceptions of a bureaucratic civil service tend to epitomize the liberal-democratic description of what political thought and action should be in the ideal case, namely, something that is informed by the appropriate scientific-technical knowledge and guided by established and neutral standards of professional behavior (which practically speaking drains the concept of any political content whatsoever). We noted that this concept of the "knowledge-based" professional civil servant seems to bear a close resemblance to Plato's own ideas about the philosopher-king and the guardian class as they are presented in *Republic*. The difference between the two, as we also noted previously, rests squarely with their respective conceptions of the individual and becomes a difference that, once it is joined with our discussion of equality, can be best described as one of diametric opposition.

From the liberal-democratic point of view, human equality means that differences between individuals are either fundamentally unknowable in any scientific *cum* systematic sense or, even if knowable, are strictly off limits to political control or guidance. Government officials, including and especially properly informed civil servants, have and should have literally nothing to do with the individual *qua* individual. Individual people as such represent a domain that is cultivated and defined by forces and ideas that reside beyond the pale of legitimate political policy and action. Freedom in liberal democracies designates the power to act within the private economic sphere, while equality guarantees that no political thoughts or actions will intrude on those of any one individual... regardless. This is precisely the reverse of Plato's position.

Let's set aside for the moment the hard and necessary questions about the limits of human knowledge, and specifically about what it is that humans can know about themselves and each other, including what it is that makes them happy and makes the social orders they live in just or unjust, good or evil. Plato's conception of politics — which designates the arena of life that circumscribes thoughts and actions of a public nature — is essentially concerned with what makes people happy and what makes it possible to say that any given political order they live in is just and good. More specifically the road to understanding and realizing such things as happiness, justice and goodness is, for Plato, one that traverses inescapably through the individual citizen. The liberal-democratic notion of equality, by contrast, requires us to bracket all individuals within a space that is homogeneously and deliberately opaque when viewed from the perspective of political discourse and activity; and, this means further and most pointedly that human happiness, virtue and justice do not require the intervention of politics and ultimately do not require the public realm either.[51]

The deep irony of liberal-democratic ideologies and the political orders they are meant to explain and justify is that the very concept of a "public realm" has become fundamentally ineffable to them. The normal Platonic inhabitants of this realm — individuals replete in their individuality — are invisible to the liberal-democratic eye because it *purposely* wears the blinding lens of a brute human equality; it sees all individuals as the same individual. The putative celebration of individuality that is viewed as the hallmark of liberal-democratic thought and practice is in fact a generalization of the highest order — every human being is the same human being — a literally un-individuated locus of pure potentiality. The ostensible virtue of this broadest of generalizations about human beings is that once it is instantiated fully and faithfully within a liberal-democratic political order, it allows each individual to become whatever it is they want to be, to become, in other words, whatever it is that will make them happy. This sounds familiar to our ears and we are even prone to embrace it in some measure if not completely. We can also see why within our liberal-democratic renditions of politics there is no inherent need for a public realm, because that realm as such really has nothing to do with human fulfillment and happiness. Political thought and action are kinds of economic activity that are differentiated from other kinds of activity only because they are instrumental in setting and maintaining the stage of individual human achievement. Insofar as politics can be said to create a public realm,

---

51   That is why virtually every political theory of the modern era (post-enlightenment on) defines human happiness at the vanishing point of politics.

this realm is really only one sector from among others that in combination constitute the overarching economic whole. The "public"
in virtually all forms of political theory that are based on or inspired
by liberal-democratic notions has no meaning or value of its own
— it is a profoundly blank and empty idea.

This contrasts fully with Plato's political thinking and also
speaks to our own often unexpressed (if not inexpressible) misgivings about what strikes us as a loss of communal or public solidarity. Even though echoes of the public continue to resonate throughout our political discourse, these echoes seem quaintly if not haunt-
ingly atavistic. The originating source of that atavistic voice (and
its echoes) can be found in Plato's political thought and, for this
reason, explains why it has disappeared from our discourse. Insofar
as Plato has come to occupy the position of idealistic-authoritar-
ian bogeyman within the constellation of liberal-democratic thinking, there seems little reason to believe that any robust idea of the
"public" that is rooted in his thinking can ever be articulated successfully. We examined in chapters one and two some of the major
reasons why the prevailing conception of Plato exists, and in this
chapter we have seen that Plato's current incarnation within the
liberal-democratic complex renders him an enemy of two of our
more cherished political beliefs: freedom and equality. In both instances this enmity stems from a configuration of the human condition that is decidedly, if not diametrically, opposed to Plato's. We
saw that the kind of freedom that liberal democracies champion
and work to secure is, in Plato's eyes, a pyrrhic effort for it achieves
its ends by stripping away everything that this freedom would be
good for... things such and justice and living well. The underpinnings of the liberal-democratic notion of freedom (what I labeled
its baseline) is a notion of human equality that is deliberately and
actively opaque so as to give the appearance, if not the reality, of
being empty; this, in turn, defines the *sine qua non* of the abstract individual. Against this Plato conceives of a political realm that is ac-

tively interested in the individual. It is precisely this "active interest" that defines the bedrock of our criticisms as well as our misgivings with Plato's thought. What falls out when we choose the equality of the "abstract individual" over Plato's notion of "active interest" in the empirical individual is, however, a coherent and working notion of the public. We will discuss in chapter four the implications of these remarks about equality and freedom. Before we do that we need to continue our examination of topics that contribute to our prevailing ideas about Plato. Our next topic is public truth, and to this we now turn.

## Truth (and Lies)

There occurs throughout Plato's writings on political philosophy the argument that under certain circumstances, and with respect to certain members of a political order, it is prudent if not necessary to tell these same members something less then the whole truth. The central reference point for this argument is in *Republic* (Book III, 414) where Socrates discusses what has come to be known as the Noble Lie. The "Noble Lie" is really a myth — a Phoenician tale, Socrates calls it — that recounts how human beings are all the same because they come from the earth, while at the same time they are different based on the kind and quality of metal that is mixed in with the earth to make them. Specifically, Socrates identifies four basic "mixing" metals: gold, silver, bronze or iron. The myth is an attempt to indicate the brotherhood of humanity (we all come from the earth) while also noting the important differences that set us apart (as philosopher-kings, guardians, farmers, or workers, respectively).[52] The myth of the metals constitutes, like the myth of the Cave, a fertile source of meanings and interpretations not all of which I intend to explore here. My interest in this myth will focus

---

52    Cf. Eric Voegelin (1966), p.105.

on what it means for political leaders to engage in storytelling of this sort, what it means to tell "noble lies."

The standard interpretation of Plato's thinking on the matter of public mythmaking is that he presents it as a device that is used by rulers to convey explanations of an uncomplicated and palliative sort to those members of the political community who are either unable or unwilling to comprehend and digest the unadulterated and direct truth. Whether and to what extent this constitutes the outright "telling of lies" is a topic of some dispute among scholars. Nevertheless it is difficult not to call this mythmaking practice some kind of lying, especially when it is set within the ideological context of contemporary liberal-democratic sensibilities. The manufacture and promulgation of a story that is not exactly or directly true, when it is executed in a self-conscious manner by political leaders who in turn know full well what the "non-mythical" story is, can find no rationale, mechanism or logic within the liberal-democratic complex of thoughts and actions that will justify it.[53] Why this is so is easy to see given our previous inquiries into the concepts of freedom and equality. If public officials within a liberal democracy know and understand the truth, then in principle all members can know it or, at the very least, should be given the opportunity to know it. As we have seen there is neither the means nor the justification for drawing distinctions among individual citizens within liberal-democratic political systems. This includes making distinctions on the basis of their intellect or their interests. All citizens in a liberal democracy are considered and treated as equal. There is no basis to argue, then, that certain things should or should not be known by certain citizens, and thus no way to justify the telling of

---

53 The simplifications or myths that one tells children before they are old enough to understand the full truth is perhaps the exception to this liberal-democratic rule, though even here one must note there are difficulties with detailing and demarcating the parameters of human development. In other words what is the developmental threshold that separates "OK to tell a myth" from "now able to understand the truth?" More importantly, do all or most adults cross this threshold and if not, why not?

stories by some citizens who are fully in the know to other citizens who are, by definition, left in the dark to some significant degree. Of course it is also true that as a matter of free choice, any citizen can choose not to know the truth or not try to more completely under-stand the truth about the political environment he or she inhabits. This willful ignorance is further based on either a lack of interest or a grant of trust to those political leaders that do in fact know the truth. The central idea is that this "ignorance" must be a decision that is made by each individual. It cannot, as Plato seems to argue, be made by the rulers for them.

Writings about the theory and practice of democracy invari-ably contain discussions about the truth and how it circulates (or should circulate) within a democratic political system and among its citizenry. These discussions tend to revolve around questions like: How much do citizens in fact know, how much do they want to know, and how much should they know? Yet in all this talk about truth there are rarely discussions about the validity and util-ity of not telling the truth or lying — noble or otherwise. The final verdict when it comes to matters such as this is that — all things being equal — if the truth can be known and is in fact known by public officials, then it can and should be told to and known by ev-eryone — *all in the same manner*. There are conceivable circumstances and situations (all things alas rarely being equal) that might make "not telling the truth" on the part of government officials a tempo-rarily prudent and defensible choice. My point, however, is that *in principle* and in the long term telling the truth is the only legitimate option for political officials in a liberal democracy. The other side of this point is that Plato is seen to be arguing for something quite the reverse of this, namely, that lying is sometimes not only prudent and necessary, but also an ethically defensible long-term policy for public officials to implement.

There are three points that can be made about how we tend to interpret Plato's justification for the telling of "noble lies." The first

I have already broached and is built upon our previous discussions of freedom and equality. Setting aside what the actual purpose or meaning of noble lying might be (something that is all-important to Plato), there is simply no theoretical basis in liberal-democratic ideology for making a distinction among individual citizens on the basis of what kinds of things they might or might not be able to know or should know about the world they inhabit, including its political component. Something that is knowable to any individual is in theory knowable by all individuals. There are numerous empirical reasons of both interest and acumen, which guarantee that in practice whole categories of truth and knowledge will not be known or grasped by a whole host of individual citizens. Nevertheless, when it comes to politically pertinent knowledge, relaying the unalloyed truth is what public officials are expected to aspire to, while each citizen is for his or her part expected to have the basic wherewithal to understand the truth — whatever it may be. The reality is, of course, that both public officials and citizens regularly dash the theoretical expectations of liberal-democratic ideology; officials tell lies and citizens remain ignorant or fail to understand what, from a political perspective, is going on about them.

The second point dovetails into the first one in the sense that the very notion of truth, and especially the "complete" or "unalloyed" truth, is obviously not one that is easily defined let alone established. To state the matter differently it is not at all apparent, and certainly not so in the case of complex political events or issues, what it means to completely or directly tell the truth about them. Liberal-democratic thought elides the gravest consequences of these problems and ambiguities by circumscribing the topics about which public truths can and should be told. And so, many of the most controversial and germane topics tend to be held out of bounds as subjects of political inquiry and knowledge. What are these "out of bounds" topics? We have already touched upon perhaps two of the most important of them. First, with respect to freedom, what does it mean to live well or what will make the individual citizen happy? Second, with respect to equality, what is each individual like, what is the empirical reality of the individual citizen? This latter point is particularly controversial because part of the dispute over the "empirical reality" of each citizen involves a precise definition of what makes up this reality. Is the reality of each individual, for example, more or less determined by his/her genetic endowment? How more? How less? The example is particularly pointed if we note that Plato's noble lie looks to be an argument for the position that humans are genetically determined at least to some significant degree (by the metals that are mixed into the earth to make them up). We need not try for the moment to resolve the specifics of these points. It is sufficient to note that enlightened political thinking and certainly all forms of mainstream liberal-democratic thinking get nervous and ultimately demure from discussions about topics like defining individual happiness or delving into the character not to say the genetic endowment (and influence) of any one individual. Instead, liberal democrats are more comfortable saying that happiness is a matter of private choice and that the specifics of one's individuality (including ones genetic endowment) are just not politically pertinent. By the same token they are inclined to see and say that Plato's political thought claims to answer — erroneously and intrusively — the question of what makes human beings happy and ultimately claims further — and even more erroneously and intrusively so — to be able to know the truth about each and every individual member of the political order. Most people today would tend to agree with this assessment, which brings us to the third point.

The ultimate irony of Plato's discussion of what has come to be known as "the noble lie," and what has come to be seen as Plato's justification for lying by public officials, is that the putative noble lie is not a lie at all. It is rather a form of telling the truth. Part of this can be explained and illuminated by our previous examination in chapter one of Plato's epistemology as it is expressed and worked out in his myth of the Cave. According to the structure of knowledge that Plato set into place in this myth, a concept like "the truth" circulates within a complicated human environment that involves both the world of light and the world of shadows as it is organized and illuminated in the cave. The latter world of shadows never truly disappears and, in fact, defines the world that we all ultimately inhabit. The story of truth for this reason, including and especially the conveyance of political knowledge, will always involve "truths" that are about and part of the shadow world, that are not in other words the complete truth.[54] But this is precisely where we do Plato so much harm. We accuse and find him guilty of trying and claiming to know too much, of trying to know the whole truth. But this claim, as I have argued, stems from a fundamental misunderstanding of Plato's thinking. Insofar as a notion like the "complete truth" exists in Plato's thinking it is represented, by way of analogy in the cave, as the sun. The fact that to gaze directly at the sun is also to be blinded by its brilliance is not without significance here. Yes, Plato argues that there is something like the complete truth, but he also argues that this truth is the functional equivalent of looking straight at the sun! All forms of truth and knowledge exist, speaking by way of the cave analogy again, because there is the sun. The varying nature of truth, which is to say the many ways that it can be expressed and the many perspectives that can be taken towards it, is directly related to the variety of human existence both in terms of the individuality of people as well as their particular interests. Any good liberal democrat will undoubtedly find little to disagree with in this pluralistic depiction of knowledge while at the same time — *and this is the difference that makes all the difference* — he/she will want to qualify this by claiming that both the specifics of our individuality and the expression of our particular interests should not be a matter of

---

54  The temptation of all utopian schemes and certainly ones spawned from modern enlightenment positions is that one can simply dispense with the shadow world and live in the light of pure transparency.

public concern, and thus strictly beyond the legitimate boundaries of politics. This difference is part of our previous discussion about how modern liberals understand the concepts "private" and "public" versus how an ancient Greek like Plato understood them. Before we explore this more fully with respect to political truth and lying, let us retrace some of our footsteps so that when we get back to this difference we can see it perhaps a little more clearly.

I think that at least some, if not all, of my readers will have been made a little uncomfortable by my claim that liberal-democratic theory adheres to a notion of veracity on the part of public officials that is so blankly (and not to say simple-mindedly) wedded to some kind of full and complete disclosure of the truth, not to say the additional claim that understanding the truth is something that is fully within the reach of each and every full-fledged citizen. We saw the same blank simplicity when we examined the concept of equality as it operates within the complex of universal public education, and we observed that at base, liberal democrats adhere to a position which holds that (under ideal liberal-democratic conditions) every citizen can become what he/she wants to become. Now to this we add the obligation that (again under the ideal liberal-democratic conditions) our public officials will tell us the whole truth with the expectation that we (the citizens at large) will in turn understand it. Of course, neither position can be said to tell the whole story.

The reader should now begin to glimpse here something that is, one is tempted to say, almost perversely ironic, namely the telling of some liberal-democratic noble lies of our own. We don't call them noble lies of course. Instead we call them ideals (even limiting ideals), something we should strive to achieve within our liberal-democratic political systems (even if they are strictly speaking unattainable). Regardless of the description or labels we give them, it can be argued that such things as open vistas of (economic) opportunity (that is, becoming what we want to become) and the high quality and broad scope of public knowledge, disclosure and discourse (that is, telling and understanding the truth) are two of liberal democracy's most cherished (let's be honest) Phoenician tales. The temptingly perverse part of this irony, however, is not that they are, like Plato's own noble lie, really a way of telling the truth — for there is an element of truth in each of them. It is that, despite whatever truth they contain, they serve to cover rather than illuminate the political reality which they are ostensibly about.

What is this political reality? It is perhaps impossible to truly assess to what degree citizens in any liberal democracy are happy, impossible to determine that they have become or are on the path to becoming, what they truly want to be within an unbridled and empowering social order. It is equally difficult to determine to what extent our public officials are telling us the truth rather than lying to us, or how much of the truth we citizens actually comprehend or simply ignore. There is, regardless, no shortage of commentary and evidence on the inequalities and injustices that are perpetrated and protected by liberal-democratic political systems, no shortage of accusations concerning the rampant and unchecked mendacity of public officials coupled with the extensive ignorance, not to say wholesale indifference, of the general citizenry. Injustices, falsehoods perpetrated by the government, as well as the indifference and ignorance of the citizenry, certainly exist to some degree in any conceivable political order no matter how it is constituted. The peculiar problem for a liberal democracy is that by virtue of its ideology, including and especially the noble lies it tells itself, topics like justice and truth are not, properly speaking, subjects of public discourse. Or rather, like the concept of "public" itself, they live as echoes in our political discourse whose source cannot be found let alone approached. It is not by accident or coincidence that truth and justice share the same ephemeral fate as the idea of the public in liberal-democratic theory and practice. They are pieces of the same story — the story that ultimately I am trying to tell. The controlling concept in this story is that of the public realm, for it is within this

arena of ideas and practices (as Plato and his fellow Greeks conceived them) that examinations and discussions about topics such
as truth and justice are supposed to happen — it is the proper (and,
according to Plato, the *only*) arena of genuine political activity.

There are two kinds of opposing comments that can be made to
what I have just stated. They can be roughly identified with the two
different sides of the liberal-democratic political spectrum. The
first, from the conservative side, is that contrary to what I claim,
topics like truth and justice are integral parts of public discourse
in a properly functioning liberal democracy. The second, from the
liberal side, agrees in some measure with my remarks about the
absence of a robust notion of public and in the consequences this
absence has on our (moribund) political discourse about issues
like justice and truth. They would question and criticize, however,
the relation I am trying to draw to Plato's political philosophy. I
plan to respond to these kinds of objections more fully in the next
chapter, where we will examine in greater detail the implications
of the interpretations of Plato that I have presented in this and
the preceding two chapters. For now I would like to conclude our
present examination of Plato's concept of the noble lie with this:
The objections brought against this concept tend to fall into two
categories. First, there are objections about the specific content of
Socrates' Phoenician tale. Treating individual citizens as legitimate
objects of political knowledge and differentiating amongst them,
even if mythically, on the basis of what amounts to (what we would
nowadays call) their natural and/or genetic endowment, is strictly
prohibited in liberal-democratic thinking by the linked notions of
the abstract individual (the "insides" of individuals are off limits)
and limited knowledge (meaning that the content and parameters
of our natural or genetic endowment cannot be known in an appropriate and politically usable manner). Second, and what forms
the more germane liberal-democratic objection to Plato's noble
lie, there is no distinction that can be legitimately drawn between

citizens that know something and citizens that don't. If something pertinent can be known by some citizens, then (in theory and all things being equal) it can and should be known by all citizens. The liberal democrat typically controls the ramifications of this claim by coming back around to the first objection and limiting rather severely the scope and content of pertinent political knowledge, a circling back that is aided and abetted by the way the liberal mind has reconfigured the concepts of public (which it very nearly effaces) and private (which it extols and grants near hegemony).

The rejoinder to these criticisms is that the truth as Plato conceives it is not a simple concept, and that political knowledge circulates and can be spoken in a variety of ways and contexts. The noble lie within Plato's complex structure of knowledge is ultimately not a lie at all but a way to express and know the truth. Moreover, we saw that the liberal-democratic critique of Plato's noble lie also contains lies or myths of its own; modern Phoenician tales that are told and, more pointedly, told somewhat out of school. I say "out of school" because, unlike in Plato's political philosophy, there is in liberal-democratic thought and practice no place — specifically no robust public place — to validate, question and/or secure the truth of these tales. This "loss of the public" is something that characterizes liberal-democratic ideologies and differentiates them from the political philosophy of Plato. The implications of this difference are a story we will unfold more fully in the next chapter. We now move to the final topic in our discussion of Plato's putative unsavory political ideas, specifically, his censorious position with respect to art.

## Art

Perhaps no part of Plato's political philosophy suffers more from the distance and distortions that tend to separate his thinking from our own than his thoughts about art and how it should be regarded and handled within a properly constituted political order. The primary culprit in this story is Socrates' presentation in *Republic* of how the proper regime for making citizens should include strict control over the kinds and content of art that each citizen both learns and enjoys. What is particularly troublesome about this portrayal is not only that it involves a very strong element of censorship; it also goes considerably beyond censorship to the point of actively delineating the form and content of art and then aggressively foisting it upon the citizenry in a differentiated manner. This all strikes the modern eye as a not too subtle effort to use art to form and control citizens. In some sense, that is exactly what Plato intends and means. It is the sense of this intention and meaning that we must now try to draw out. It can be said from the beginning that Plato's designs are not as nefarious as they appear, while our own revulsions and indignations are not as innocent as we think.

Some remarks about Plato's conception of art, especially as it occurs in the context of *Republic*, are close at hand and do provide some mitigation for what we have come to see as his promulgation and defense of the active control and use of art by public officials. First of all, Ancient Greek culture tended to treat what we would consider serious art forms as activities that were rightly and fully folded into the functions of state. The public festivals that were held to perform tragic and comedic dramas and award prizes for the best ones are perhaps the most obvious examples of this strong connection between art and politics. Secondly, the scope and content of art tended to be less broad and less highly differentiated than what we nowadays mean by the word "art," in particular what we would now call "fine art." Indeed, our whole taxonomy of art with its distinction between "fine" and "applied" versions does not match up directly or easily with the ancient Greek taxonomy, which tended to treat all art as "applied" and differentiated among forms of art primarily on the basis of their function. Because art "did something" in the ancient Greek conception of things, the notion that public officials might be directly concerned with what art was in fact "doing" was not as strange or untoward as it might seem to us. This is especially true with respect to Socrates' discussion of how the state should control and use art in his presentation of the just polity. The "art" that Socrates identified specifically was actually a composite regime of "art forms" which we would identify today as poetry, music and gymnastics.[55] It is the teaching of these three things, in combination, that Socrates was most keen to delineate and have his political officials understand and ultimately control. This three-part educational regime implicitly mirrors the various tripartite structures in Plato's philosophy that we identified and discussed in chapter two. For example, and most directly, the psyche of the individual, which is composed of some integral arrangement of mind-spirit-body, was to be nurtured and developed by the "music" regime of poetry, music and gymnastics respectively. To bring our stories full circle this regime is nothing less than the educational regime that Socrates would recommend for "life in the cave," and ultimately a life lived at its best. The end product of this strict educational regime is that for some members it will result in the *periagoge* (the turning) towards the light. This helps explain a less noted yet significant feature about Socrates' discussion about the "music" regime he proposes, namely, that it becomes more intense and more controlled as it goes up the educational status ladder. The regime that will cultivate and educate future philosopher-kings employs the most highly controlled use of art that Socrates presents. This fully inverts what is the normal conception of how, for example, totalitarian or paternalistic regimes might seek to use the arts to influence and control the citizenry at large (which is to say, to use art as propaganda). It should be noted as well that this use and control of art as largely pedagogical engaged individuals in the manner of a practitioner rather than as a passive observer

---

55 The transition from the applied arts of the Classical Greeks to the fine arts of our own time can be seen in the fact that what Socrates identifies as gymnastics (what we would now call an applied art and sport), has become *qua* art more appropriately identified in our day as dance.

or interpreter of art. At its most intense, namely in the training of future philosopher-kings, we observe a regimen of doing things and not mere thinking or contemplation. It was not a regime that would be concerned primarily or even secondarily for that matter with observing, understanding and criticizing art — which conforms more to our own aesthetic conceptions. This emphasis on practice is integral to the Greek way of looking at art forms in a functional manner. In this particular case art was meant to work on the entire *psyche* (mind-spirit-body) of the individual; Socrates' pedagogical regime (poetry-music-gymnastics) recognizes that turning from the world of the shadows, and understanding and seeing the differences between appearances and reality, requires what I have called the "full body turn." It is not a mere mental exercise, not a mere molding of thoughts and ideas. It can be further noted, in anticipation of some objections to my argument, that even in the case of art as a wider public event, as in the holding of public festivals, the characteristic ancient Greek view of such events was inflected toward the participation and public functionality of the festival rather than the appreciation and assessment of individual artistic achievements.[56] This is not to say that the Greeks failed to appreciate and judge art along an aesthetic register, or that they appreciated and judged art only in mere functional-utilitarian terms. It is to say that the act of appreciating and judging individual works of art and individual artists occurred necessarily within a rich context of public participation, discourse and finally, functionality.

Even when we take into consideration these mitigating observations there seems to be a substantial remainder of concern about Plato's use and control of art. The remarks we have made in our previous three discussions about freedom, equality and truth provide ample reason for why this is so given the way that liberal-democratic theory defines the human condition. The control and use of art by

---

56  The festivals are, foremost, forms of public celebration that seek to unite and educate citizens, and even criticize (if somewhat obliquely) current political events.

public officials for public purposes would clearly result in laws and policies that are strictly forbidden by any truly liberal-democratic government. The very idea that art could be used by public officials for public purposes and not at the same time be tainted is nearly unimaginable to the liberal-democratic way of thinking. The one and only thing that liberal democracies can do legitimately with art is to foster and support its production, without any concern for its content beyond the normal caveat that any given work of art not explicitly threaten or directly destroy the very framework that allows for its creation. The fault line between free artistic expression and harmful mutations of it such as pornography, propaganda or even "attacks" upon the state itself defines an active and mobile territory of contention and controversy. This "zone of conflict" between art and its negative "others" is left deliberately undefined, both in terms of its boundaries and in terms of the ideas and practices that are employed to contest and adjudicate specific instances within it. The variety of liberal-democratic opinions about what constitutes art, as well as the empirical examples of how actual liberal-democratic political orders define and delineate art as distinct from its perverse, harmful or unacceptable forms, spans a broad and rich continuum that is, albeit significant to the thought and practice of particular liberal democracies, unimportant in our discussion of how it compares to Plato's political philosophy.

The core of this comparison is that against what is ostensibly an open and contentious notion of art and its expression, there stands Plato's more closed and fixed ideas on the matter. The strong emphasis that Plato places on the public utility of art requires that he curtail and even direct individual artistic expression. The justification for this involvement is that it is conducted under the auspices of "knowledgeable" public officials, most notably under the direction of the philosopher-king. The boundaries and guidance that said public officials give are rendered legitimate because they are to play a central role in making the political order a just one, as well as the people who live in it happy and good. This strikes the modern liberal-democratic ear as at best merely a verbal formula that cannot possibly be realized for a host of reasons, the most important of which being that there is no knowledge about justice, goodness and happiness that can be known and implemented in the way that Plato imagines. Here we can see a recapitulation of our three previous discussions, where the control and direction of art is not only a fetter on free artistic expression but requires that the foundation of these fetters be found in the specific truth of each individual. The artistic training regime that Socrates describes is based fully on knowledge of concrete individuals and is a knowledge that specified what art is good for which citizens. The value of art is unequal for Plato because citizens are unequal in their empirical individuality, that is, in their ability to understand and use and benefit from art. This actual individuality, though not categorically denied as such by any liberal-democratic creed, is at the very least beyond the reach of the instruments of any legitimate liberal-democratic state. By virtue of the notion of the abstract individual — a notion that counterintuitively generalizes rather than individuates — each citizen is substantially responsible for creating and defining his/her own truth, which is to say, responsible for locating and developing what constitutes his/her goodness and happiness. This includes the specific responsibility for defining his/her individual relationship to the creation and enjoyment of art in all its forms. Finally, then, we see as well that Plato's noble lie (that people are both the same and different) was required so that, among other things, public officials could legitimately control and direct art. In the same way, liberal democracies are fundamentally tied to their own (ig)noble lie that each and every one of us can become what we want to become and in doing this can achieve happiness (including, by implication, determining what part if any art will play in this achievement). A political system that facilitates and allows this achievement (and stands clear of art as best it can) is what renders it a just one in liberal-democratic eyes. We have seen on a number of occasions how close liberal-democratic ideology comes to Plato's own views, and this notion of the realization of happiness within a just political order is no exception. Once again, however, the difference between them makes all the difference.

In our examinations and discussions of freedom, equality, truth and now art, we are always brought to the point where Plato's distinct and fully articulated notions of a public (political) versus and private (economic) realm of human existence are altogether different from liberal-democratic views that tend to subsume the entire human condition under a rubric of private *cum* economic choices, actions and structures. Under this latter rubric we see that concepts like public and politics are ultimately reducible to their more elemental private and economic components. This difference between Plato and liberal-democratic ideology becomes particularly marked in the case of art, especially in our notions of fine art. There are two interconnected reasons for this.

The first involves the value of art. It is a commonplace that genuine works of art are in some measure priceless, that no amount of economic value fully captures the truth and beauty that is embodied and expressed within a work of art. The second involves the irreducible "public" dimension of all forms of arts. According to this view, art realizes its meaning first by being publicly displayed or performed and finally by being publicly appreciated and validated. Modern liberal-democratic societies, because they lack an independent notion of public and instead drive everything through the grist mill of private-economic life, tend to distort and displace the non-economic and inherently public dimensions of art. Genuine art may be priceless in some sense (and it will be that sense that we will examine in the next chapter), yet in our globalizing, economically driven world there is a value (a price) that can be assigned to everything including any and all manner of art. As concerns art's public dimension the two art forms that perhaps best characterize the liberal-democratic sensibility, the novel and the cinema, are at first glance nothing if not fully "privatized" art forms. We read novels and see movies essentially in private, and we appreciate and validate them by an aggregation of individual approvals that turns them into bestsellers and box offices successes respectively. I will argue in the next chapter that, far from being completely "privatized," the novel and the cinema are in fact sublimations of a need within human social existence for a vigorous public dimension. For now I will note that it is precisely this sublimation of a public dimension in art that informs the visceral distaste we have for Plato's political philosophy, a distaste that reaches its apogee in his proposals to use and control art for public purposes. Under the conditions of a sublimating process, no amount of mitigating and contextual argument will wash this stain from his philosophy. To put the matter more bluntly, art is all liberal democrats have to bind themselves together as human beings and it is as such the only source of critical distance and traction against a conception of political thought and practice that is (invidiously) hegemonic, ironically because it is putatively so "open and tolerant."

***

I have argued in this chapter that Plato's political philosophy is not as bad as we think and that our own liberal-democratic theories are not as virtuous as we believe. The normal response to an analysis such as this, especially if one is a good liberal democrat, is to use it as a corrective to liberal-democratic thought and practice and then move on. In my view, this is not what happens next because the differences between Plato and the modern liberal-democratic outlook are fundamental and not easily or readily conjugated one to the other. The rub is this: We cannot simply discard Plato's philosophy unless we are also willing to discard certain conceptions of goodness, justice and happiness. Conversely, we cannot handle and achieve certain forms of goodness, justice and happiness without paying heed to what Plato's political philosophy tells us... a telling that is incidentally distilled in his Cave myth.

## Chapter 4. Sailing Back from Syracuse

It is rather ironic that a philosopher who has achieved a reputation for being a "head in the clouds" idealist should have been actually so engaged in the real world he lived in, up to and including the end, when he tried, unsuccessfully, to educate and turn the tyrant of Syracuse into a more benign and beneficial king...if not some kind of philosopher-king. One can imagine a rather poignant moment when, sailing back to Athens for the last time from Syracuse, an evident failure, Plato contemplates the intractability of the human condition in relation to the palpable beauty of the sunset upon the Mediterranean horizon. What manner of world could hold all these things at once? Even a mind as lucid as Plato's must have bent to the rush of incomprehensible thoughts and emotions that so great a contrast would put into play. One imagines further that at some point he simply shook his head, turned from the rail of the ship and went below.

\*\*\*

I have argued so far that the commonplaces about Plato's political thought, including their more sophisticated academic variants, tend to be fundamentally distorted by what I have broadly construed as the dominant political ideology of our time, liberal democracy. Parts of how this distortion has come about have been touched upon in the previous chapters. Nonetheless, a comprehensive historical account is beyond the scope of my present analysis.[57] That analysis has instead focused primarily on trying to see a different Plato than the one most of us are accustomed to seeing, and this change of perspective has offered up some intriguing slants on the ideas and practices associated with liberal democracies. I have, however, pulled up far short of taking a full measure of what this "different" Plato might have to say about our contemporary political environment. Perhaps another way to say this is that even if one were to admit and concur that Plato's political philosophy has been misinterpreted and misrepresented along a broad band of the modern political spectrum, and by a large assortment of thinkers and commentators who populate that spectrum, it is still not clear what a more sympathetic and different reading of Plato's political philosophy will in the final analysis accomplish. Many of the obvious problems with Plato's philosophy — that it is anti-democratic, excessive in its claims to know the truth, and finally not an evident recipe for human goodness and happiness at all — seem to remain valid despite whatever mitigating inflections and twists of interpretation are brought to bear upon them. It seems that even when Plato is seen in a different and more accurate (not to say sympathetic) light, most of us still don't like what we see. In this chapter I will try to examine and explain what importance a revised interpretation of Plato's philosophy might have for our contemporary political condi-

---

57  I would argue and have argued above in chapter two that Christianity, first by way of Augustine, plays a major role in inflecting and distorting our understanding of Plato's philosophy. Ostensibly, starting with the Enlightenment, Western political philosophy has sought to purge itself of it's sectarian *cum* Christian influences and components. This has not been as successful as many claim... but that is a topic for another time.

tion and well-being. Ultimately the task at hand is not about under-standing Plato "better" or getting him "right" (whatever that might mean); it is about understanding our political situation better and making our individual lives better and more (humanly) rewarding. Only if Plato's thought can help us do that will it warrant greater attention and deeper study. Otherwise it is of value and interest to the antiquarian only.

In my examination of Plato's philosophy so far I have looked at three elements. First, in chapter one, I examine the Cave myth, which I have claimed is about the character of human existence at its most fundamental and unalterable level. The appearance-reality dynamic that constitutes the core theme of the myth is an aspect of human existence that is, according to Plato, both central to it as well as in some sense beyond dispute. To argue otherwise is to mis-understand and distort what the human condition is about, though it should be noted from the outset that misunderstanding and dis-tortion are, given the very appearance-reality dynamic that Plato maps out in his myth, a part of the human condition that cannot be fully eradicated.

Second, in chapter two, the more ambitious argument is made that the fundamental nature of the appearance-reality dynamic im-plies that the structure of the world (the cosmos) be of a certain sort. For Plato this structure must not only include what he identifies as mind (nous), but must do so in a way that maintains the compre-hensive unity of the cosmos. I use the term "comprehensive unity" here to explicitly distinguish Plato's position from, on the one hand, that of modern science which tends to posit a unified natural world, but is acutely (if often mutely) unable to square its conception of a monistic natural world with the reality of the self-conscious human beings who live in it. On the other hand, it distinguishes Plato's position from "people of faith" who assert the existence of a tran-scendental realm or entity beyond nature that is, in some manner, not only not a part of this world but also not something that human reason can rightly fathom — hence the need for faith.

Finally, in chapter three, I examine the topics of freedom, equality, truth and art as these concepts are differently understood and/or deployed by Plato versus what I have called the liberal-democratic complex. If it can be rightly argued that human beings and the cosmos they inhabit are continuously enacted within a mutually constructed and sustained context, then we see that our current context is greatly influenced if not dominated (especially at the ideological level) by liberal-democratic thoughts and practices, and it is these thoughts and practices that delineate such areas of human interest and value as freedom, equality, truth and art. It is these delineations conducted under the very auspices of our liberal-democratic outlook that render up the predominantly negative assessments we have of Plato's political thought and give us the "bad Plato" of our common understanding.

In this chapter we will work our way back to the Cave myth first by way of an extension of the previous examination of the topics of freedom, equality, truth and art. This discussion will focus on the different and divergent conceptions that Plato has of the public and the private realms, including their interrelationship versus those that prevail within contemporary liberal-democratic thought and practice. This difference offers a fundamental lever that can be used to critically examine the ideas and practices of any and all liberal-democratic ideologies and the political systems they underwrite. The pivot point of this leverage is the resonance of a (one is tempted to say atavistic) belief in the idea that social orders, and the political systems that minister to them, are somehow and in some way concerned with issues of substantive justice and goodness. This concern cuts two ways — first in terms of individuals and what it means for them to live well, and second in terms of political systems and what expectations are placed on them in order to aid and abet the achievement of individual wellness and/or goodness, and in consequence of such achievements attain as well some level of social justice. It will be argued that this concern with issues of sub-stantive justice and goodness cannot ultimately be supported by any theory that is a participant in the liberal-democratic complex. The ramifications of this concern acquires whatever significance it is likely to have only insofar as we remain committed in some significant measure to issues of substantive justice and individual happiness. This concern (or lack thereof) then becomes the lynch-pin of an argument that ties Plato's ideas to our ongoing interests in justice and human happiness (or not). Thus, if we decide to roundly jettison Plato's political philosophy (that is, in effect, to remove the lynchpin), then we run the risk of losing our ability to defend, handle and sustain *in a rational manner and within any kind of public context* a whole host of ideas and practices that are concerned with justice and well-being. The starting point for either alterna-tive — "lynchpin in" or "lynchpin out" — is the myth of the Cave. If Plato's thought is to remain tied to our own — if we are to remain somehow devoted to questions of justice and goodness — then we have to reconsider what the myth of the Cave tells us about our own essentially liberal-democratic ideas and practices. Alternately, if we choose to forgo Plato then we must reconsider what takes the place of Plato's fundamental myth.[58]

## Public and Private

It is something of a commonplace to observe that modern life tends to be dominated by questions and concerns of an economic sort. The political fortunes of governments and their leaders, espe-cially liberal-democratic ones, are increasingly tied to indicators of economic performance and well-being, while individual citi-zens themselves are swept along by prevailing economic currents towards ever greater levels of productivity and consumption. The

---

58 I have already suggested that one alternate myth could be the Garden of Eden story.

general contours of this description as well as its overall (global) applicability can of course be disputed either in whole or in part. Governments do face and consider questions and concerns that (at least appear to) trump economic issues, and it is certainly true that not all, or even most, people are solely (or think they are solely) driven by desires to make and spend more money. However one chooses to understand the place of economics in the modern world it is, despite any qualifications we wish to draw up and place upon it, difficult not to locate it somewhere close to the very heart of contemporary human concerns. It needs also to be kept in mind, however, that our understanding and use of the term "economics" is far different from Plato's understanding and usage in certain significant respects. Plato's idea of economics, as noted in the previous chapter, tends to be broader than our own as well as more tightly differentiated from politics as a separate sphere of human activity. The foundation of Plato's ideas about economics and politics is set down in the way he divides and assigns value to the human condition.

The difference between how an ancient Greek like Plato looked at and valued the world and how a modern liberal democrat (or even more broadly speaking any post-enlightenment modern thinker) looks at it can be stated relatively easily but it is difficult to fully comprehend. The source of this incomprehension is more than a simple misunderstanding and even more than a matter of historical distance. It might best be described as a function of anthropological engineering — a matter, in other words, of the kinds of people we have made of ourselves coupled with the kind of world we have fashioned around us. [59] The tragic element in the historical trajectory that has taken humankind from the Athenian *polis* to

59   I am using the term "world" in the same way that Arendt uses the term as something that is made by and inhabited by human beings. In this way it is to be distinguished from the cosmos, which is the "natural world" that provides the setting within which the human world emerges. Arendt (1958).

our emergent global economy is that it does not seem to have been accompanied by any discernible amount of increase in our understanding of ethical and political matters. In other words, much has changed, but not necessarily for the better. Indeed, aspects of what we are likely to consider "better" remain locked in the past — the ancient Greek past — and they continue to haunt and animate our needs and desires even though we struggle with the ability to faithfully express them, not to say realize them in any remotely adequate fashion. Plato's conception of the public realm and the political activity that occurs within it are at the center of this struggle. It is a struggle that is at once a source of yearning in our hearts and stolid silence in our heads. Why is this so?

The ancient Greek taxonomy of political order holds that politics and economics refer to two separate and quite distinct areas of human interest that are each linked to a separate sphere of human activity, one designated by the term public and the other by the term private. In a well-ordered society, political activity would occur in the public realm while economic activity would take place in the private. Societies become disordered when the two spheres of activity become mixed, and specifically when private interests are authorized and appropriated as part of the public interest. And thus, for example, the difference between a king and a tyrant for an ancient Greek was that the former ruled in the public interest while the latter did not and, rather, treated his kingdom as if it were his own private property. None of this sounds too controversial at first blush. We can appreciate that political activity conducted under the auspices of the "public good" is duly legitimate while activity that serves a private interest is not, that it is instead a misguided, even wrongful political activity. This agreement between ancient Greek thinking and our own is relatively superficial and masks what are some significant disagreements about what in detail constitutes a well-ordered society. There are two peculiarities in the classical Greek account of social order that can help us understand what these disagreements are.

First, the manner in which societies became disordered for the ancient Greek was asymmetrical in that it always came about when private interests were promoted by means of political actions taken in the name of the public. Within this scheme political activities and their consequences could be called right and just only if they were informed by the public interest. These activities became wrongful and unjust as soon as they strayed from the public path into the surrounding areas of private interests. These private interests were wrong and unjust, however, not because they were inherently evil or bad (though they could be that but only incidentally so) but purely because they stemmed from private rather than public valuations. Recall that the divide between public and private and, in turn, the very substance of the distinction between politics and economics, was for the Greek essentially a function of the difference between citizens and households. Citizens, their collective actions, and their communal well-being constituted the public sphere. Households, each taken individually, constituted a sphere of private interest and activity, which in some very strong sense could not have any collective identity whatsoever. Insofar as they could be referred to collectively at all, it was only under the constitutive rubric of the political entity or entities to which they happened to belong. The common denominator that ties public and private spheres together was ultimately citizens who so happened to be members of the public sphere as well as individual households.

The second peculiar aspect of the classical Greek taxonomy of social order was the ambivalence it betrayed with respect to the political form of democracy. The origins of democracy are generally and undoubtedly rightly attributed to the ancient Greeks. It is, nonetheless, a matter of some curiosity if not concern that the two greatest Greek political philosophers, Plato and Aristotle, had

a difficult time characterizing democracy in anything but a negative light. It's almost as if for either of these thinkers any democracy was a political order in some degree of disorder. We touched
upon why this might be the case briefly in our discussion of the
topic of freedom in chapter three. We saw that democratic political systems tend to break down the difference between the public
sphere and the individual spheres of private economic interests that
collectively reside within the boundaries of a given political order.
Why this breakdown should occur may not be immediately evident,
since (to our way of thinking) if a king can both rule as a king or a
tyrant (that is, either for or against the public interest), then why
can't the people at large (the demos) do so as well? The answer can
be found in the deep-seated functionalism that underwrites both
Plato's and Aristotle's political thinking.[60] A Society for them was
well-ordered when the people who governed it knew what they
were doing, and this "knowing what they were doing" was linked
directly to finding and serving the public good. There is an art if
not a science to politics, and like any other human endeavor one
must learn and practice it in order to do it well. All democracies
invariably fail at this because no one in a democracy has the time
(as Aristotle would have it, the leisure), training or inclination to
do politics *qua* politics; because, in addition to delving into political
matters periodically, citizens are working at some other "private"
vocations full-time.[61] The one thing that each member of a democra-

---

60   For an example of Plato's functionalism see Book X 601 d5

61   We should note the differences between the Greek conception of democracy based on elections by lot and what has become in modern liberal-democratic systems a representative democracy that elects public officials. Representation appears to answer the objection about officials in
a democracy being functionally committed to public rather than private
interests. However, the solution is only an apparent one as the "special interest" character of contemporary electoral politics clearly demonstrates.
Whether you have democracy by lot or democracy by representation, the
outcome is ultimately and eventually the same; both fail to address the crux
of the problem with democracy... the existence of a realm of interest and
value that stands apart from individual private interests. Kingships and ar-
istocracies ostensibly do address this issue insofar as they are — by virtue

cy does know well (because in some sense no one cannot but know it) is his/her own private interest.[62] And so, for Plato and Aristotle, what happens in a democracy is that private rather than the public interests are promulgated by the political system, and to their way of thinking this leads to some degree of "disorder" — *and consequently, to a political system that is inherently unjust.*

Consider conversely how the liberal-democratic temperament is wont to describe both the sources of disorder and the merits of democracy. As concerns disorder, the issue for the liberal democrat is not that a society becomes disordered when its leaders serve private interests; rather, it becomes disordered when the political system itself and its actions get in the way of the pursuit and satisfaction of private interests, either by privileging some private interests over others, or even more problematic and likely, by becoming a source of interests in itself. That a political system could become an interest unto itself is for the ancient Greek outlook flatly incomprehensible, while for the liberal democrat it is the *sine qua non* of the dark side of politics.[63] This complete reversal of the etiology of disorder explains the liberal-democratic defense of democracy as the "best" political form — as the form most likely to make our individual lives good and our political orders just. Democracy is defended as the political system most likely to promote and secure our private interests in a fair and equitable manner, while at the same time insuring that public authorities do not undermine this process either in the name of some interests over others but especially in the inter-

---

of the economic freedom that kings and aristocrats enjoy — able to uncouple themselves from private interest and govern with the public interest in mind. This informs Socrates' elaborate and radical discussion of the fiscal and social arrangements that underpin the guardian class, arrangements that only make sense as a guard and check against the intrusion of private upon public interests.

62   This should not be confused with knowing what is best or good for the individual.

63   See note 61 above — the very transition from "democracy by lot" to modern representative democracy explains the mechanisms by which public officials can derive and become an interest unto themselves.

est of government itself. What falls out of the liberal-democratic account of social order and disorder is the notion of a public realm as a place that is distinct from private spheres of activity and, more importantly, as a source of activity and interest that is not directly derived or composed of interests that come from or act like private interests. Plato's and Aristotle's misgivings about democracy make no appearance in this conception of things. Quite to the contrary the source of their misgivings — that democracy is essentially a framework for the pursuit of private interests — is converted within liberal-democratic ideologies into its overriding value and virtue.

What does it mean for the public realm to fall out of the liberal-democratic account of political order? Liberal-democratic ideology and discourse are after all full of references to the public. So, how can we say that it's "not there?" The term "public" of course still appears in all kinds of liberal-democratic discourse. It is rather the meaning of this term that is substantially abbreviated from Plato's use in that it does not refer to a realm of human thought and activity that exists substantially apart from the private realm. Instead it is derived from and composed of private desires and interests that are (mostly willy-nilly) protected and/or promoted by the government. These desires and interests achieve their status as "public" ostensibly because they are identified by the will or voice of the people. The "people" in a liberal democracy, however, as we have previously noted, are little more than individual citizens whose insides are, when considered from the very perspective of the liberal-democratic theory that establishes them, basically empty. Individuals "get filled up" (and voice their interests) as members of groups or households within private-economic spheres. Nothing inherent to the public-political sphere is allowed to determine what goes into the insides of individual citizens. As already seen, this is in fact what liberal-democrats mean by human equality: Everyone is empty or is treated as if they were empty. And what they mean by human freedom: Everyone is free to judge and determine what fills them up."[64]

Plato's account of the public realm differs from that of liberal democrats in that once a political order is formed, that is, once private households are joined together within an overarching governing regime, the public sphere is brought into being in a way that constitutes a locus of thought and activity that is *sui generis*. Indeed for Plato, not only was this public realm substantially separate from the private spheres that brought it into being, it formed a realm of thought and action that was normatively superior to the component privates spheres that it ultimately sheltered, protected and maintained. The nature of this superiority was partially a function of its capacity to do justice, but even more importantly it was superior to the private realm because it embodied the very conditions under which justice can be known and achieved. Plato's stern assessment of our political landscape would be that without a duly acknowledged and functioning public sphere (as he understood that term) there can be no genuine human justice, and without justice of this kind a very important element of human goodness and happiness becomes no longer achievable.[65] It is precisely at this point that the lynchpin that either ties Plato's political philosophy to us or not is located.

---

64  Kimlicka (1989) defends liberal democracy against criticisms that it is based on abstract individualism and value relativism. I don't claim, however, that liberal democracies believe in either abstract individualism or value relativism as Kimlicka presents these notions. My point is that in terms of the ideology or theory of liberal democracies, nothing is substantively asserted about either the individual or about the social order he/she inhabits. My point is that all variants of liberal democracy relocate questions about what individuals are and what they value within a private-economic *cum* individual bucket (even when this bucket is itself contain within a bigger biological or societal one). These questions only get put into any kind of public-political bucket by being poured directly from the (more logically prior) private-economic one(s).

65  I am making a distinction here between what I would argue is the true nature of political justice, which is essentially substantive (concerned with concrete results) and that of economic justice, which is primarily procedural in nature (and essentially concerned with keeping the economic engine chugging along).

As we have noted, most normal liberal-democratic responses to Plato's notions about justice and goodness tend to be that much of what he identifies as just and good does not strike us as either particularly just or good, and that those things that remain desirable political or individual goals are better achieved by other (which is to say liberal-democratic) means. A large part of the preceding analysis has been an effort to set the groundwork for analyzing this two-part claim in greater detail. Part of the problem, as we have tried to demonstrate, is that many common understandings about Plato are inclined to prejudices that tend to distort his thinking precisely in those directions that we have taken it and in the process make him look bad. Still, we cannot cash this demonstration out unless we can also show that this prejudice has important consequences for both our collective and individual well-being, unless we can demonstrate, in other words, that there are things that Plato identifies as collective and individual goods that cannot be achieved by liberal-democratic means. This demonstration will lead us back through his philosophy, his structure of the world and ultimately... back to the Cave.

## Good Plato

In chapter three we discussed four topics that tend to give Plato's political philosophy a bad reputation. Two of these topics, freedom and equality, are cornerstones of the liberal-democratic creed while for Plato they are either irrelevant or downright misleading. The other two, truth and art, tend to define areas of human activity that are highly valued but held at arms length by the liberal democrat while they play a central functional role in Plato's thinking. The simplest way to describe this difference between liberal democrats and Plato is to say that the key sphere of human existence for a liberal democrat is economic, while for Plato it is political activity within the public sphere that is central. What this simple description tends to leave out is that whereas Plato duly recognizes a private sphere that exists apart from the public, the liberal demo-crat subsumes the public sphere within the general ambit of the private and treats it as one species of private activity from among many others.[66] Within the liberal-democratic scheme of things, Plato's political ideas become unacceptable if not downright scary because they get applied throughout the entire spectrum of human existence (and this is precisely why a critic like Popper could ac-cuse Plato not only of being anti-liberal, but also of being a kind of proto-totalitarian). But Plato's "political" reach does not actually go beyond a certain point. Though it is true that he gives pride of place (that is, normative superiority) to public rather than economic life, he does not conflate or combine the two spheres of human activity. While it is also true that what happens in Plato's "public realm" has consequences for the entire social order, this is true no matter what. It is true for the liberal democrat as much as it is true for Plato. The key question (or so Plato would have it) is: What kind of political influence do we want to have on our collective lives and then, by implication, on our individual lives as well? If Plato tends to fright-en us it's because he insists that we have this choice and that we need to be serious about making it. The liberal democrat makes us feel better by telling us that this public responsibility is really only our private responsibility (read: freedom) writ large. This however is deeply misleading.

Let us return for a moment to the ancient Greek taxonomy of or-der and disorder. Societies, as we discussed, are well-ordered when they are ruled by and for the public good rather than private in-terests. The good king is distinguished from the tyrant because his rule is focused on nurturing public value, while the tyrant simply treats his kingdom as if it were his own private property. Democ-racy represents a problem in this taxonomy because it equates the public good with private interests. A liberal democrat is naturally inclined to ask: But what's wrong with that? What makes so-called

---

66   In the language of philosophy Plato draws an ontological distinction between public and private while liberal democrats do not.

"public" actions based on private interests unacceptable? In the case of the tyrant the problem is obvious enough. When a tyrant acts his actions are, from the perspective of his subjects, capricious and arbitrary (based on his own internally generated — which is to say private — ideas and interests). Yet, the critical problem with all privately informed uses of power, no matter what the source — king, oligarchy or the people — is that it is inherently and unavoidably willful and arbitrary (that is, internally and not publicly generated). Whether this power is exercised by one person (a tyrant) or everyone (the people) makes no difference in this regard; it is still essentially arbitrary. Indeed when liberal democrats discuss the problem normally called the "tyranny of the majority," they are no doubt saying more then they know. The liberal democrat is wont to argue that the difference between tyranny and democracy, including democratic tyranny, is that in a democracy, we do it to ourselves. Regrettably (and admittedly) this "ourselves" may not include significant minorities within the political order who happen to disagree with the majority view. Liberal democrats have responded to this challenge in a variety of ways, but all of them can be categorized under the description of "protecting or defending minority rights" from the abuses of majority power. From Plato's perspective, the troubling thing about this putative solution to the "tyranny of the majority" is that it effectively elides it. It conceals what is the essential issue at hand, namely, the arbitrary use of power as such. Political actions, according to Plato, that are not grounded in some notion of the public good are by default actions that are grounded in private interests. The real issue with the tyranny of the majority is not that when we (the so-called people) do it to ourselves, this "ourselves" does not contain everyone. This is only a symptom of the problem. Rather, the real problem is that, even if the "ourselves" did contain everyone, that is, even if there was virtual unanimity about doing something, the "doing it" would still be arbitrary and, most significantly, the effects would be necessarily uneven. The hard fact about the exercise of power in a liberal democracy is that *over time* private power becomes unevenly distributed and the effects of that power unequally felt. Some liberal democrats may (and do) want to argue that this unevenness and inequality should be mitigated but they entirely fail to see that to argue for mitigation is to turn in the direction of Plato.

Let us consider once again the extreme endpoints of the liberal-democratic complex. Both libertarians and communists deal with the problem of arbitrary political power, not surprisingly, in much the same fashion: they make it go away. What is less readily understood is that all versions of liberal-democratic ideology are pulled in either the libertarian or the communist direction. No matter which "extreme" direction a given political system tends towards, the normative end remains the same: the state withers away and mankind is emancipated from the arbitrary use of power.[67] Libertarians and communists are easily dismissed as utopian idealists because they are frank enough to follow their profound distrust of arbitrary power to its logical conclusion.[68] The problem with this dismissal is that it fails to acknowledge both the underlying attraction that each extreme utopian vision holds on the liberal-democratic imagination and, even more importantly, it masks the still fundamentally arbitrary uses of power that characterize any and all liberal-democratic governments.

Liberal democrats will of course find this conclusion difficult to accept, but this difficulty arises not because it is wrong but because it is well hidden. The veil which hides it is knit from yarn that comes from four varied and in some respects opposing sources. Foremost

---

67   There is a slippery slope of sorts for both social democrats on the one hand, who are pushed towards ever wider and invasive uses of government involvement, and conservative liberals on the other who in their enthusiasm to reduce the size of government are moved to invest ever more in the hidden "wisdom" of free-markets.

68   What Habermas and others identify as a "legitimation crisis" is precisely this inability to found then explain the uses of political power in a way that makes it no longer arbitrary, no longer some expression of private interests. Cf. Jurgen Habermas (1975).

among them is the concept of free and open markets. Under this notion many of the arbitrary uses of power in a liberal-democratic social order are transmuted by the impersonal workings of markets that collect and collate individual desires and actions and churn out results that are determined by no one in particular. The guiding hand of these markets is invisible not because it can't be seen, but more so because it does not exist.

Closely linked to free markets are the "police" powers that are exercised by the political authorities in order to maintain the putatively neutral framework of freedom, which predominantly includes "free" markets, and provides the structures within which individuals pursue their own individual or group goals. This use of police power is considered "merely" procedural and, when it is done right, promotes or protects no interests over any other.

The third strand is the intrusion of transcendental — which in most cases is to say religious — values and interests into our political discourse and practice, and while these interests have a determinate "source," that source is revealed rather than arrived at through any form of rational public argument or discourse within a duly designated public forum. Because of their fundamental and acknowledged (if not boasted) non-rationality, transcendental *cum* religious values and interests are as arbitrary as any values or interests that humans individually (and internally) generate. Indeed from a humanist or nonsectarian perspective (including most assuredly Plato's) religious values and interests are privately generated interests and values of a particularly virulent sort — because they carry the weight of God.

Finally there are the original ancient Greek concepts themselves, such as politics, public, justice and the good, that still resonate throughout our political discourse. These ideas are linked to values and interests that many liberal democrats (especially of the humanist/nonsectarian bent) consider to be the primary defense against and mitigation of private interests and the arbitrary power that is

exercised on their behalf. However, as I have tried to argue and demonstrate, these venerable ancient Greek ideas live a rather phantom
even distorted existence within the liberal-democratic complex of
thoughts and practices. Revitalizing these ideas, I contend, must
involve a reexamination and reclamation of Plato's political philosophy. We have conducted a good part of the reexamination; now let
us begin to see what it may mean to reclaim Plato.

## Plato and Freedom

As I have already noted, the concept of freedom played little or
no part in Plato's political philosophy. There are both theoretical
and practical reasons for this absence which are in fact mirrored
in contemporary liberal-democratic thinking as well. As we saw in
our previous examination on freedom, there are serious (perhaps
even insurmountable) and arcane issues with the concept of freedom that have animated philosophic inquiry since the beginning of
the Christian era, if not before. The controversy tends to be muted
in Plato (and in fact most ancient Greek philosophy) by an overriding concern with the discovery of what constitutes the good and
happy life. That a human being could and would choose actions
that would ultimate lead to goodness and happiness was in some
measure looked upon by Plato and his fellow Greeks as a kind of
background assumption to human existence. The mechanics of freedom — "Are we free to choose?" — were not as critical as whether
there was something we could call the good and whether (and to
what degree) humans could know it. Plato, accordingly, wedded
his theoretical inquiry into the concept of the good with the practical issues surrounding how the good could be known and by whom.
The myth of the Cave, with its portrayal of the appearance-reality dynamic, is about this relationship between knowledge of the
good and the knower of the good, primarily the philosopher. To a
strong degree, then, the central issue for Plato's political philosophy was not whether humans could and ultimately would choose

the good. The good, strictly by virtue of what it is, is something that people would choose by definition. This strong link between "knowing the good" and "doing good," however, seems difficult to square with what we know about human beings and how they act. Critics of Plato's position are quick to point out that humans all too often choose and do things contrary to what is good for them, even when they know it. These criticisms of Plato miss their mark because knowledge of the good was not for Plato a kind of once-and-for-all syllogistic event; it was rather an ongoing existential process.[69] Within the entirely appropriate imagery of Plato's Cave myth, knowledge of the good and doing good happen in front of the wall, which is to say, happen in the world of shadows. It is true that turning and moving up towards the light (and ultimately the sun) provides a philosopher the opportunity to contemplate goodness, but at some point in the process the philosopher must turn and go back down to the world, must go back into the cave. The important point that critics of Plato miss in this journey up to the good and back is that the philosopher cannot stay up with the good, nor can he "physically" bring it down into the cave for other fellow humans to enjoy. The good and human existence are in two different places and are related in a complex interchange that Plato seeks to convey by the structure of the cave and the movement of the philosopher within it. This complex and mobile relation between the good, the philosopher and the world (of shadows) demarcates the core of Plato's political philosophy and makes his lack of concern with freedom intelligible. It is also true however that some working notion of agency is presumed by Plato, otherwise his concern with the good and justice would not make much sense.

Liberal-democratic thinking shares with Plato both the presumption that human freedom exists, as well as the inability to give a detailed and compelling theoretical account of it. Unlike Plato, however, who places freedom in the background, liberal democrats

---

69 In fact Plato explicitly indicates that the good is not "compleletely" knowable, see Book VII 533a5.

draw it to the forefront of their political ideology. It is not hard to see why. Freedom is the one good or human value that liberal democrats are able to gain consensus on because it is, like the abstract individuals who exercise it, a good without content — an open-ended potentiality that achieves its broad acceptance among people because it places nothing substantive at risk. It is, moreover, around the value of freedom that the entire armature of the liberal-democratic political system (the framework of freedom) gets built and legitimized. There is disagreement among liberal-democratic thinkers as to whether anything like "the good" actually exists beyond the particular good of freedom. Even amongst those liberal democrats who do acknowledge that something beyond the value of freedom may exist, there is disagreement about whether and under what conditions it can be known. Regardless, the controlling notion for any liberal democrat is neither the good itself nor knowledge of that good (as it is for Plato); rather, it is that all determinations and decisions about goodness (and happiness), no matter what their pedigree, must pass through the gauntlet of the (freely choosing) individual.[70]

It is precisely this emphasis on the individual that people find most attractive and compelling about liberal-democratic thinking. At the same time it is this emphasis that seems to create an unbridgeable gap between individuals and the different kinds of social groups they belong to or identify with. In the liberal-democratic literature this is normally identified as the problem of community, specifically, of how to establish the reality and legitimacy of values

---

70  Some critics of liberal-democratic ideology (who call themselves something other than liberal but which I include within the liberal-democratic complex) focus on what is thought to be the inherent value relativism of a strict liberal-democratic position. Thus they distinguish themselves from "liberal-democrats" on the basis of their belief that something like goodness exists and can be know in a way that exists above and beyond what individuals say it is. The problem is that these critics and their putative "liberal-democratic" adversaries all generally still adhere to some notion that — whatever goodness is — it is the individual that must acknowledge and validate it.

and interest that arise from social entities that are larger than the freedom bearing (and freely choosing) individuals who make them up. Although the "political" community tends to be viewed as the *primus inter pares,* other communities (cultural, religious, biological and vocational) play an important part as well amongst competing thinkers on the matter. The bridge that is invariably built by liberal-democratic thinkers (including many of their critics) is constructed from such things as knowledge, discourse and consensus. In other words, the truth and legitimacy of communitarian values is established and granted in a liberal-democratic context by individuals who know things, talk about those things and ultimately reach some measure of agreement or consensus concerning them (even sometimes if this means agreeing to disagree). Of course the deep ambiguity that surrounds any formulation of this sort can be evoked by two questions: One, where does this bridge building actually take place? What space does a liberal-democratic political system put in place to provide for this activity (when in fact the liberal-democratic inclination is in the opposite direction)? Two, what are the mechanics by which individual decisions are translated into these legitimating social outcomes? That any description of individuals who are investigating, discussing and agreeing about truth and values sounds idyllic is more a symptom than the cause of this ambiguity. The root cause of this ambiguity is an inability or unwillingness to draw distinctions among different kinds of social forms, including the "all-too-different" individual people who belong to them. The truth appears to be that, within liberal-democratic theory, building bridges of consensus and legitimacy from individuals to the outside social world is something that can happen everywhere and be conducted by everyone — which logically speaking is a lot like saying it happens nowhere and is conducted by no one.

Plato's position on the relation of the individual to the greater social order is far more specific because it is mediated by actual concrete political activity. The distinction we find in Plato's political philosophy between the public and the private realm gives him, moreover, the basis for creating a locus where this political activity could take place. This distinction is doubly significant. First, it sets the public and its interests apart from the teeming disorder of private interests and tastes. It establishes by means of this separation a realm that is not devoted to expressing or satisfying private interests and instead would be concerned with finding and expressing ideas and actions that promote justice and the public good. Second, it conceives of political activity as something quite distinct from actions whose ultimate purpose would be to promote, protect or adjudicate private economic interest. The primary focus of political activity in Plato's view is justice, and justice cannot be achieved by, for example, promoting hard-pressed causes or adjudicating irreconcilable disputes. That is more akin to how liberal democrats conceive of justice, where politics is used to fine tune and facilitate the overall aggregate (individual) results of a teeming economic sphere of activity (the central operators of which are markets). Within Plato's political thought the public realm is the place *and only place*, and politics constitutes the activity *and only activity* which in combination make justice possible — or to say it even more directly: they are the place and activity that produce justice.

The notion that justice is "produced" rather than, say, discovered and then cultivated may seem at first glance a peculiarly inappropriate way to describe Plato's position on the matter. We are generally inclined to think that, given Plato's ardent idealism, justice is for him something that is "out there" to be known and that, once it is known, needs to be implemented and administered within a political system. Isn't that why, after all, when a political regime is ruled by a philosopher-king it is the best and most just political system? Our analysis of the Cave myth demonstrates that such a simple transfer or compression between what is outside the cave (the sun *qua* the good which is the basis of justice) and what happens in it (the shadows *qua* human existence) is not an accurate description of what Plato is trying to show us. Indeed the structures of the Cave myth (the shadows, the fire, the wall, etc.) and the philosopher's movements within and among these structures (turning, going up, and going back down) are an argument against the very kind of simplistic idealism that critics identify as Plato's position. The interpretive framework that is usually foisted upon Plato's philosophy is, as we discussed in chapter two, more Christian than Greek inspired; for nothing characterizes this standard interpretation about what was going on in Plato's thought better than the Christian idea of Incarnation — the Word become Flesh. Unless we choose to ignore the Cave myth, however, not only is any kind of "incarnation-type" interpretation of Plato's position wrong, it is dead wrong.

That justice is "made," then, is a more appropriate description than it appears at first blush, and certainly when we consider the full implications of Plato's Cave story. There is, in addition, the aforementioned functionalism of Plato that makes more sense when justice is set within the context of a locus and an activity that brings it about — in other words that produces it. Plato (as well as Aristotle) talks about the art *(techne)* of politics much in the same way as we would talk about any kind of art or craft, namely as an activity that produces something on the basis of a specialized knowledge and set of skills. There is a very strong sense in which Plato intends this to be an accurate depiction of what politics and the people who engage in political activity are about — and the product of this political craftsmanship would be justice.

Modern liberal democrats are ironically both sympathetic and hostile to this notion of politics as a particular functional craft or profession. The basis of this Janus-faced opinion is the scope of what this functional category takes in. As we saw in chapter three, liberal democrats are sympathetic to the idea of a science-based "public administration" that is founded on the knowledge, competence and experience of expert government officials. But the scope of these types of decisions is strictly constrained by what these putative government experts can know by way of science-based empirical methods. And, amongst the things that fall outside of this scope of knowledge are precisely those things that Plato would not only include, but would place at the very core of what the *techne* or profession of politics is about. And, at the hub of this core he places the concrete individual and his happiness — an entity that is strictly off-limits to the thoughts and practices of liberal-democratic politics — which brings us once again to the concept of equality.

## Plato and Equality

If freedom is the central value of liberal-democratic politics then equality is the primary mechanism by which this value is cultivated and harvested. Equality in the liberal-democratic lexicon has, as we have noted previously, two distinct but interconnected meanings. First, there is the overall general notion of human equality (all men — and now women as well — are created equal) that provides the brute parameter and foundation for the concept of the (empty) abstract individual; and second, there are the more specific administrative and legal structures that the political system implements and maintains to insure that the "framework of freedom" does not intrude on the individual, and thereby gives all citizens the maximum opportunity to pursue and define their own happiness and goodness (filling the emptiness up). A political system that maximizes freedom by way of enhancing and even enforcing equality is, according to the liberal-democratic view, a just system. It is important to note that a just political order such as this does not automatically result in the happiness and/or goodness of individual citizens. Rather the justice of a liberal-democratic system resides in the fact that it provides the best opportunity for individuals to achieve and live a life that is happy and good. Whether one's life is or is not actu-ally happy and good is ultimately up to each and every individual.[71]

This liberal-democratic "sequence of events," that is, from free-dom to human equality to justice (via political equality) and ulti-mately to individual opportunities for happiness and goodness, is plainly different from how Plato thought about social order and justice. He links together (if not equates) the justice of a politi-cal system with the happiness and goodness of its citizens.[72] This linkage means that a political system and its officials must be ac-tively interested and involved with the "insides" of all its citizens — which is to say, involved with and interested in their happiness and well-being. The initial liberal-democratic reaction to anything like this is that any measure of intrusion by a political system is a limit on freedom (a clear indication of how freedom and equality are tightly bound in the liberal-democratic mind). One needs to set aside for the moment the temptation to simply draw the conclusion that when a political system and its functionaries are interested in the individual (which within our analysis means treating people as different, not equal), the result is necessarily a manifestation of au-thoritarian repression, and furthermore under the correct techno-logical conditions, an invitation to totalitarianism. There is, first of all, the separation that needs to be made between Plato's theoreti-cal point — the idea that knowledge of the good is possible — and the practical implications of that point when one tries to "bring it down" to the real world (or what within the cave imagery is the

---

71 The sources of goodness and happiness vary and, as we have seen, the institutions and groups that constitute what liberal democracies call civil society are the primary source of how an individual will come to define his/her happiness and goodness. Despite this, the controlling element in this operation remains the consent of the individual. How much initiative or self-searching the individual puts into the process is up to the individual. The political system for its part seeks to insure that neither it not any part of civil society is permitted to foist on the individual their views of happi-ness and goodness.

72 Practically speaking, one cannot blankly equate justice with happi-ness or goodness because fate and luck interfere with real life in ways that often change and determine outcomes from what in theory they should be.

world of shadows). In other words — if all one takes away from Plato is that he posits that in a just political system public officials know what is right, and ordinary citizens need to listen to and obey them for that reason, then one has not understood the irony that stands behind his thinking. As in the case of Socrates — truly the wisest of all men who ironically imparts nothing that can be directly or overtly identified as wisdom — a just political system is actively interested in what makes each of its citizens different, not because it can or even should speak (let alone determine) what that difference is, but rather because it knows that this difference exists and to act as if it does not — which is to say to treat everybody as equal — is a kind of injustice or maltreatment of a most invidious and misleading sort.

Plato's political philosophy is like liberal-democratic theory in that it is ultimately based on the individual. But unlike the typical liberal-democratic thinker he is concerned with the concrete rather than the abstract individual. He is interested in what people really are, which includes a concern with what they have been and what they will become. Indeed the sum and substance of political action undertaken in the public sphere was, for Plato, that it take a direct interest in the well-being of the concrete individuals who make it up. If the political order fails to do this, justice and human happiness are inevitably truncated, deprived of their crowning value register. As we have seen, the liberal-democratic calculus of value is decidedly different from this. In liberal-democratic thought the just political system protects and facilitates individual and/or group activity so that it can (hopefully) lead to individually decided and defined versions of happiness and well-being. The problem with this conception in Plato's eyes is not, as one might expect, that it results in a veritable gumbo of definitions about human happiness and well-being. Indeed, Plato's emphasis on the concrete individual requires that human happiness and well-being be defined and realized in a variety of ways, and one by one. The problem with liberal-democratic individualism is rather that it does not and cannot work the way liberal democrats think it works or even could work.

Any definition of human happiness and well-being within human society must in Plato's view be tied to a working notion of justice. This in turn requires a fully functioning and robust public sphere — something that I have argued all liberal-democratic thought and practice lacks and ultimately cannot supply. Liberal-democratic political systems for this reason do not recognize nor can they ultimately establish a genuine public sphere, and by implication they do not conceive of political activity as inherently distinct from other forms of privately delineated human actions. For the liberal democrat it is quite literally butcher, baker, soldier, sailor... and politician. This stands in direct contrast to Plato's philosophy. He defines politics as those activities which order society. The character and quality of a social order in turn define whether and to what extent a political system is just. The public sphere and the political actions taken within it are for Plato, then, qualitatively different and normatively higher than the economic sphere and the private activities that happen within it. Politics has a vaunted normative status in Plato's thinking not because (or only because) it is merely "better" than any other kind of (private) activity, but rather because without it the entire collection of human activities (public and private alike) becomes in some significant degree disordered, hence unjust and finally a limit (literally a devaluation) on the entire spectrum of human happiness and well-being. *Individual happiness and well-being, the good of each individual, cannot be systematically realized (that is, realized across the entire aggregate of citizens and over time) without the justice that political action delivers by way of activity within a public sphere.* Insofar as particular "private" individuals achieve any kind of happiness and well-being within a disordered political system, this achievement is the result of a fortuitous combination of fate, ability and/or luck.[73]

---

73   This is the same manner of explaining how Socrates comes about.

The inevitable, yet hidden and denied, trajectory of any liberal democracy as concerns the matter of justice and individual happiness is some form of Social Darwinism. Socrates characterizes all societies that are not ordered by politics but bent more by the interests of private individuals as a city of pigs. The point of this derisive epitaph is to draw the distinction between what makes human society — where justice is the highest good — different from animal behavior *per se* (social or otherwise) — where interest is defined by desire and instinct and cashed out by power, strength and luck.[74] Within our modern nomenclature a city of pigs can be characterized as a society that provides for the survival (read: happiness and well-being) of the fittest, where "fittest" is further defined as those who best adapt to their particular environment (an adaptability that is granted primarily or solely on the basis of fate, ability, talent and luck). The real effect of freedom and equality as defined by liberal-democratic ideology is that some number (and most often this is the greater number) of citizens will not thrive (flourish), but will fail in varying degrees to successfully adapt to and engage their economic environment — and this despite whatever "political" decorations (echoes) liberal democrats choose to hang on it.

---

74    Plato's use of the term "city of pigs" occurs in Book II 372d. The actual reference is attributed to Glaucon as a response to Socrates' original formulation of the "just" *polis*. Some readers may find my use of this term here dubious, if not gratuitous, in that it may not be clear how this original "just city" is linked to Social Darwinism. What links Plato's city of pigs with Social Darwinism is that both are expressions or depictions of natural justice. Plato deploys this portrayal in order to demonstrate the limits of natural justice; specifically, that natural justice does not equal human (political) justice. He uses the city of pigs as his first step towards the truly just city. Liberal-democratic ideology actually reverses this process in some sense by making a city of pigs its ultimate destination. Consistent with some of the things that were said in chapter two about Christianity, as well as some of the concluding remarks I will make in chapter five, there is, in the liberal-democratic vector towards natural *cum* Darwinian justice, a deep attraction for the paradise that is the Garden of Eden — which is, like Socrates' city of pigs, a depiction of unthinking, instinctual, natural justice.

A conclusion such as this will invariably be resisted tooth and nail by any and all manner of liberal democrat. The varieties and arcane steps that liberal-democratic thinkers take to avoid or miti-gate the effects of their inherent Darwinian logic never do the trick, however, because this logic is hard-wired into the anthropology of liberal-democratic thinking. Liberal democracy can never truly jus-tify the kinds of actions that must be taken by a political system to help people when they "can't survive" or succeed on their own. There are no conceptual resources or practical measures that allow the liberal democrat to say: "In order for this individual to be happy the political system will have to help him/her in this or that way." The only kinds of help the liberal democrat can rightfully extend are prologues and preconditions for self-help. Any measures that reach beyond this "self-help" limit are at once illegitimate (*qua* political), and thus best characterized as based on some kind of pity or char-ity. This explains why the ongoing legitimacy of all forms of social welfare in liberal democracies is fundamentally precarious — they can come and go, and at any time, for they have no basis that serves to justify their existence. It also explains how these programs are deeply demeaning to those unlucky souls who must rely on them to survive. It is Plato's insight that human happiness and well-being require that we see and respect each and every individual for what they really are, that we see and engage the concrete individual and not some abstract notion of that individual who, when given the proper initial starting point, or even the occasional helping hand, will achieve his/her own well-being and happiness.

## Plato and the Truth

In our discussion in chapter three of Plato's noble lie we saw that, far from being a plain and simple falsehood, the noble lie was actually meant to convey, in a certain manner and to a certain audi-ence, the truth about the brotherhood of human beings as well as their individual differences. The fact that this noble lie may harbor or convey the truth in some less than direct manner is not enough to save it from the criticisms of liberal democrats who see in it an unacceptable measure of duplicity and as something that unnecessarily comes up short of the complete and unadorned truth. There are no grounds within liberal-democratic thinking for pointedly speaking the truth in different ways to different people. And here the distinction must be drawn between, for example, pedagogical uses of myth (or "lying") — where it is used to help someone make their way towards an understanding of the truth (which a liberal democrat would condone) — and Plato's intention to convey the truth by way of myth, and in some measure and to some citizens only in that way. As Plato's myth of the Cave implies, turning from the shadows to the truth almost certainly cannot happen to everyone in the cave.[75] This differentiation between people is precisely what liberal-democratic thinking cannot forgive (as our discussions of equality have shown) and it informs their rejection of the concept of the Noble Lie. All prisoners of the cave for the typical liberal democrat — based on their abstract equality — must be free and able to turn towards the light. Conversely, it is the differences between people — in effect that not all of the cave dwellers will in fact turn or even be able to turn — that inform Plato's concrete individualism as well as his use of the noble lie.

We can better understand this difference between Plato and liberal democrats on the subject of the character and quality of truth telling if we once again remind ourselves about Plato's functionalism. According to Plato's functional perspective, politics is a specific field of knowledge and activity that, like any other, cannot be universally understood or practiced by each and every human being to the same depth and degree. Some combination of talent

---

75  Plato provides no number for how many "prisoners" in the cave can be set free though he clearly implies that the notion that all of them could be set free is extremely unlikely... and it is unlikely for the very simple and unassailable reason that human variation (based on the dense confluence of natural endowment and environmental context) is a biological-ecological fact.

and inclination set limits to what individuals can and do know about different spheres of thought and practice including politics. Neither Plato nor a liberal democrat, for example, would criticize a physicist for writing in a "less than truthful manner" about his field of interest and knowledge to a more general (non-specialist) audience. It is not considered objectionable when a physicist simplifies or bends the truth in order to impart some measure of the truth to an audience that cannot comprehend it any other way. The difference when we move to politics is that Plato envisions it as a field of knowledge that is like physics or any other field of specialized learning and skill, whereas liberal democrats do not. Politics is, of course, for Plato a particularly important field of knowledge because of its highly esteemed subject matter — but it is a specific field of knowledge nonetheless. And, the notion that the truths of politics can (or even should) be known by any and all citizens would make no more sense to him than the idea that each and every citizen become even remotely as knowledgeable about physics as any well trained and competent physicists.

Liberal democrats certainly do not credit Plato's ideas about politics as a "specialized" field of knowledge, at least not in terms of what each and every individual needs to know and be able to do as a fully functioning citizen in a liberal democracy. They assume instead that each citizen can, in theory, know and engage in politics as well as any other. We have already discussed why, from Plato's perspective, citizens of a democracy are able to know and perform their duties as citizens since in a democratic political order the primary area they need to know and care for is that of their own private interests. On this point, liberal democrats and Plato are in agreement. It is when we move from private interests to matters of justice that, as we have also previously discussed, Plato would break ranks with liberal-democratic thinking. A democracy cannot achieve justice, cannot be considered a truly just social order according to Plato, because it is at best an aggregation of private desires and interests that more often than not are a reflection of some combination of the more powerful, talented and/or fortunate of its citizenry. As we saw in chapter three it is the "Phoenician tales" of liberal democracies — their own noble lies — about such things as public disclosure and discourse (that is, speaking and knowing the truth), as well as about self-realization within a free and empowering economic sphere (that is, liberty and the pursuit of happiness within open and free-market structures), that aspire to reveal the ideal truths or goals behind actual liberal-democratic practices, when in fact what they actually serve to accomplish is to hide the truth about the falsehoods and injustices that inherently pervade and propel liberal-democratic political systems forward.

This a bitter pill, so bitter in fact that even though most liberal-democratic thinkers see and understand it in some measure (they see falsehood and injustice in existing liberal democracies by the score), none can bring themselves to swallow it whole. Instead, the liberal-democratic response can be divided into three general camps which can be labeled for our purposes as utopian, minimalist and realist. The utopians search until they find some mechanism or conceptual recipe that will render ideals such as truth and "equal" opportunity real (Marx, a utopian of great historical insight, regrettably found his answers in Historical Materialism). For the utopian there lingers the belief (or hope) that there is some way to develop and organize a society so that it is both fully transparent (all people can see the truth) and, because of this very transparency, consistently and broadly just. Exactly what will make said society "just" eludes the utopian as it eludes any liberal-democratic ideology. The descriptions of justice in such utopian societies are generally a re-enactment (or restatement) of the Phoenician tales they are meant to realize.

The minimalists agree that liberal democracy has many faults, including some manner of distorting the truth both about telling and knowing the truth, and about what the actual results are of "free activity" and the pursuit of happiness as it occurs within putatively open market structures. Yet they argue that any other set of principles or form of political organization will be far worse. The best that can be done is to pragmatically tinker with the liberal-democratic machinery so as to minimize mendacity and ignorance as well as delimit power and wealth and even at times redistribute it. One might call this the Churchillian or pragmatic response (liberal democracy is not the best form of government but it's the best alternative from among all the others we know or can think of).

Finally the realist will acknowledge that some people will not know the truth and will not achieve goodness and/or happiness, yet in the end that is their own fault. Each one of us is ultimately responsible for the knowledge we have and (to put it in the correct realist idiom) our for own economic/private success. This we might call the Augustinian response... which often, if not understandably, cushions the harshness of its outlook on the human condition with the mercy and love of a divine being, as well as the promise of a better (and more just) life in a transcendent "other" world (the irony of this escapes many of us).

In practical terms all minimalist liberal-democratic ideologies will eventually gravitate to the kinds of policies that the realist position from the outset articulates and defends (that is, some manner of Social Darwinism which is hard-wired into the liberal-democratic view of the human condition). At the same time there will always be the temptation to succumb to the utopian wish to mitigate the harsh and ultimately mindless effects of the realist position — but these mitigations, which can come in any number of forms (ranging from public welfare to private charity), lack any staying power because, as we have seen, they lack legitimacy (liberal democrats can't really explain why such mitigations are justified). Even more importantly, they are fundamentally demeaning to the people who receive them, because ultimately and according to the liberal-democratic canon, each of us is responsible for our own success or failure. If you need public welfare or private charity then you have failed, and the fact that this welfare or charity exists is not because you need it and certainly not because you deserve it. It exists rather because those who have succeeded (the powerful, the talented and the lucky) have decided to extend it to you — a bitter pill, indeed.

It is the sophist Thrasymachus who in Plato's *Republic* plays the part of the realist and identifies and defends the notion that justice is in the interest of the strongest. Few liberal democrats, regardless of pedigree, will of course openly identify themselves with the likes of Thrasymachus.[76] Instead they will raid the cupboard of classical Greek political concepts — justice, virtue, public and good — and hang them on the armature of their fundamentally Darwinist ideology and call it good. The point to be noted about Socrates' criticism of Thrasymachus (and of the sophist he engaged in some of Plato's other dialogues as well) is that there is one sense in which justice is indeed in the interest of the strongest. The sense in which this is true is in the natural sense, meaning that if we forgo a definition of justice that is tied to our humanity for one that is based on our (animal) nature, then the justice we achieve will be the natural justice of animals (Socrates' city of pigs and Darwin's law of the jungle).[77] The homing beacon of all liberal-democratic thought is this "natural" city where justice is defined by and in the interest of the strongest. This beacon is well hidden by both the aforementioned (not so) noble lies that liberal democrats tell themselves and by the use of originally ancient Greek notions like justice and the public good — notions that come to us in phantom form. It is Plato's claim that a truly human definition of justice — one that defines and aligns justice with some idea of the good — must understand and come to

---

76    If I may be permitted a bit of contemporary political commentary, the thoughts and actions of today's so-called neocons *qua* Straussians strike me as more Sophistic than Socratic. It seems that many of the current generation of Strauss's putative "disciples" have done for him what others in another time did for Machiavelli (or even what Elizabeth was able to do for her by then mute brother).

77    See footnote 74.

terms with life in the cave. This in turn would help us understand and come to terms with the truth that stands behind Plato's noble lie: that people are the same *qua* human but quite different *qua* individuals — and it is the latter difference that political justice must recognize and serve. The typical liberal-democrat can't get there, can't get his/her conceptual arms around the Cave and the concept of justice it underwrites.

## Plato and Art

We discussed in chapter three how Plato's conception of art differs from our own liberal-democratic notions. Part of that difference is that Plato's views, as with his views of politics, tend to have a strong functional component. This makes his ideas about art more narrow and focused. They are in this way more like our ideas about the applied rather than the fine arts. Indeed, it can be claimed with some measure of justification that the modern distinction between fine versus applied arts was flatly incomprehensible to Plato.[78] It can be further claimed that when we refer to art, it is really only fine art that we have in mind. The applied arts are to our way of thinking more readily relegated to the areas of crafts and artisan skills. This "post Plato" distinction between applied and fine arts begins to explain why modern critics are so put off by Plato's political philosophy (an off-putting that reaches its climax in the Socratic effort to delineate and control art in the just political order of *Republic*). We also noted, however, in our previous discussion on the topic of art that a deeper (in this instance sublimating) logic is at work in contemporary ideas about art that helps further explain the liberal-democratic reaction to Plato's views, especially as they are expressed in *Republic*. It is this deeper logic that will concern us now.

---

78   For Plato, discussion of art as applied rather than fine see starting at Book X 596 b.

The importance of art in the liberal-democratic mindscape is at once both easy to miss yet difficult to exaggerate. If anything can be said to be sacred within this mindscape it is the practice and enjoyment of (fine) art. It is the individual creative artist and his/her unencumbered works of art that have earned a kind of sacred place in the liberal-democratic scheme of things. As part of this (quasi) sacredness, art defines an arena of human activity that is strictly off-limits to official political interference. Plato by contrast does not treat art as anything sacred at all. Rather he reserves this distinction for the public realm itself, and for the political thoughts and actions that occur within it. Art for its part is related to the public and politics as more a means to an end — the end being the just polity and the well-being and happiness of its respective citizens. Such an instrumental relation between art and politics will tend to strike the contemporary sensibility as inappropriate, even (and not surprisingly) sacrilegious, as something that goes completely against the grain of what art (namely fine art) is supposed to be.

Perhaps we can gain some insight into the differences between Plato's ideas about art and our own if we take a look at the structure of artistic activity in general. Within all artistic activity there is a linkage between a work of art and truth that is forged by the knowledge and skill of the artist. It is furthermore this transmutation of truth by means of the skill and knowledge of the artist that ultimately determines whether, as well as to what degree, any given work of art can be called beautiful or not. This three part linkage — between truth, the knowledge and skill of the artist and beauty — applies across the entire spectrum of human artifice — sculpture and poetry as well as cabinet-making and animal husbandry. The kinds of "artifice" that come within the specific ambit of official control in Socrates' discussion of the just *polis* are primarily those kinds of artistic activities that have a public dimension or influence. Poetry, music and gymnastic have a pedagogical role to play in developing citizens and leaders, while the more obvious public arts, like the performance of plays or the construction of public spaces and buildings, can assume a whole host of roles such as providing information and comment on current events, or simply celebrating and reinforcing the common bonds of community and citizenship. In all cases it is the "ordering" effects of an art form that make it important to Socrates' discussion of the just city. We can now see that the "beauty" of the pedagogical arts that Socrates details in *Republic* — the interconnected musical regime of gymnastics, music, and poetry — resides precisely in their ability to "make" well-ordered, which is to say beautiful, souls. There is no inherent beauty or value that resides within the individual art forms themselves. Rather, their beauty derives from their functional excellence, from their role in making virtuous, well-ordered citizens. In the same way, and consistent with Plato's application of the man-city analogy, the performance of plays and the building of public buildings or monuments (architecture) are to the *polis* what the pedagogical regime is to the individual. The "beauty" of these civic art forms is seen to reside in how they contribute to the development and maintenance of the well-ordered and just city, and not in anything inherent or unrelated to that contribution. Such tightly drawn functional connections between art and the production of good character or justice are difficult for the liberal democrat to appreciate let alone accept. It all seems unseemly in its proximities to politics and vulgar in its blatant functionalism. And yet, the liberal-democratic conception of art — which is, to repeat, fine art — is not all that different from Plato's functional conceptions. The connections between truth, character, art and beauty are all there — they are just relocated and reconfigured. The major operator in the displacement and reconfiguration of art is the loss of a robust and independent public sphere and, consequently, a loss of the political actions (literally the making of character and justice) that should occur within that sphere. In the liberal-democratic mindscape art becomes unraveled and "falls away" from our now absent public space and politic activity. The irony of this unraveling movement is that it actually can be seen to begin in Plato's own work as he comments and reflects on the disordered state of Athenian politics.

We noted that it is the public realm and political action that hold the normative high ground in Plato's political philosophy. But, what happens when a political order becomes so disordered that the public realm disappears and politics becomes virtually inoperative? This is a question that confronts Plato, not theoretically, but empirically. The challenge to Socrates represented by the Sophists and ultimately by his trial and death is Plato's dramatic theoretical portrayals of what he identifies as the degeneration and ultimate destruction of the public sphere and politics in the Athenian *polis*. The question that all these portrayals allude to in some way is: When a *polis* is so disordered that political activity and the public sphere become inoperative or unavailable, what happens to them? The answer is that they are forced underground — they, and the human interests they serve, become candidates for some manner of sublimating and/or relocating process. In Plato's thought it is philosophy and philosophers that represent and foster a kind of underground public and politics. And his justification and explanation for this choice can be found in the myth of the Cave, which in turn (as we have argued) assumes a certain kind of structure of the world — in particular a world which contains mind *(nous)* as a distinct ontological reality. Plato's efforts in this direction become derailed for a variety of reasons, not the least of which is the emergence of Christianity as a source of an anthropology and cosmology that is distinctly if not directly opposed to that of Plato's and his fellow Greeks.[79] This derailment sets into place a historical sequence that results (among many other things) in the sublimating of the public and politics. Not, as Plato would have had it, into the discipline of philosophy and the person of the philosopher, but into the area of the fine arts and the creative activity of the artist.

---

79   This is discussed in detail in chapter two.

We can situate the preceding points on art into a larger context as follows: Within liberal-democratic ideology we observed that political activity loses the special normative status that Plato attributes to it and becomes repositioned, within the larger private *cum* economic sphere of human interests and activities, as primarily a set of laws and practices whose central purpose is to maintain the overall framework of private economic actions (what I have called the framework of freedom). One of the by-products of this repositioning of politics is that it makes it difficult for us to fully appreciate the kind of value that Plato places on political activity and the public sphere. Another more subtle by-product is that the human interests and values that, for Plato, are served by politics and located within the public sphere become re-channeled and re-defined into other activities, all of which happen within the over-arching (and essentially undifferentiated) sphere of private life and economic action. A major manifestation of this re-channeling can be observed in the emergence and status of the fine arts (and the creative artist) as a field of activity that is awarded a special and vaunted (if not sacred) status.

Before we discuss the meaning and significance of (fine) art as it pertains to liberal-democratic ideology, it will be helpful to take a brief look at how Plato's political philosophy conceives of and handles religion. Plato's views on religion have received far less critical attention primarily because the religions of ancient Greece were pagan and polytheistic. A whiff of the exotic and even the primitive accompanies religions of this sort, and this certainly helps account for the lack of *gravitas* when it comes to what Plato may have said about the topic. His views on religion, however, are unsurprisingly much the same as his views on art.[80] Like art, the religions of ancient Greece were tied to their respective political systems in a manner that is far more intimate than what we are accustomed to seeing in our own time, even in instances, for example, when there is an

---

80  Indeed, art and religion are two categories that are not readily separated in ancient Greek thinking. But that's a topic of discussion unto itself.

established religion that is supported by the state. The key factor in making it difficult for us to understand the nature of ancient Greek pagan religion (or Roman religion for that matter), and how it related to the political order of which it was a part, is again the emergence of Christianity. We find in Christianity the creation of a set of institutions and practices that were from their inception separated from any political order as such. This separation was captured by the idea of the church — a notion that really has no counterpart in Plato's conceptual universe.[81] Whereas the primary focus of the institutions and practices of a church were and remain the individual and his salvation, religion, as Plato understood it, plays a more fully functional role, again like art, as an "instrument" of the social-political order.[82]

Religion is used in this way to convey knowledge, primarily in the form of comprehensible "noble lies," and to develop and reinforce (through acts of piety) the character and well-being of citizens while at the same time to legitimate and reinforce, by way of religious festivals and ceremonies, the solidarity and cohesion of the political order. The more stark distinctions we would draw between art and religion are altogether fuzzy for someone like Plato. As with Plato's notions about art, the ostensibly blatant and "official" instrumentality that informs his ideas about religion tends

---

81    The closest analogues we would have to how pagan religions functioned in Plato's time are political systems like Nazi Germany, Stalinist Russian or Maoist China. These systems deployed pagan-like practices: the cult of personality, state pageantry and the overt presentation and celebration of national (and party) symbols. It is interesting that in these modern examples the creation of what amounts to a sublimated version of a pagan state religion is predicated on the disestablishment and suppression of existing religious institutions (churches) and practices. The history of religion in the West as it moved from paganism to Christianity and beyond is certainly a rich subject, especially in terms of how this history influenced and was influenced by political thought and practice. That history, however, is well beyond the scope of the present discussion.

82    It is not incidental of course that both Christianity and liberal-democratic ideologies have the individual as their focal point. I have already argued in chapter 2 that our (mis)understanding of Plato is primarily based on the Christianization of his philosophy.

to set our liberal-democratic molars on edge. Nevertheless, liberal-democratic theory is characteristically ambivalent about religion and certainly about what has come to be known as organized religion. Religion can be and has been used as an instrument of the state, while at the same time it has been and continues to be a source of individual spiritual enrichment and development. Part of the liberal-democratic ambivalence towards religion can be explained by observing that in the historical movement from ancient Greece to our time, the ideas and practices of religion, much like those of art, also began to "fall away" from the public sphere and political thought and action. Thus, Plato's notion of religion as tightly bound to the *polis* and functionally focused on pedagogy and social cohesion gradually gave way to a concept of religion that circulates more independently from the state and, by virtue of this independence, interacts with individuals on a private rather than public basis. The significant difference between religion and art on this score, however, is the aforementioned emergence of Christianity and the concomitant establishment of institutions and practices of (primarily Christian) churches that stand apart from the political orders they inhabit. The consequence of this is that, quite unlike the case of art, the public form and political function of religion as Plato conceives it has been *openly* redefined and relocated rather than subjected to any kind of more oblique sublimating process. The liberal-democratic ambivalence towards religion is based on what, from Plato's point of view, would be the overt creation of institutions and practices under the rubric of organized "churches" that stand in direct competition with those of the political system proper. Insofar as any church tries to unduly influence or control individuals, such efforts run squarely up against the liberal-democratic values of freedom and equality. How far these "political" values reach into the ideas and practices of organized churches demarcates a zone of ambiguity and controversy with which liberal democrats have continuously wrestled. Whereas the history of western political philosophy has, since the emergence of Christianity, included a power struggle between "church and state" that has been partially resolved for the time being by their "official" separation, no such overt struggle or resolution has accompanied the history of art.

Liberal democrats are ambivalent about religion because it has in some measure become, especially by way of institutional Christianity, a kind of state within or even "above" the state. Art has no such liability (or advantage, depending how you feel about institutionalized religions). Indeed it is somewhat misleading to talk about art as having any kind of institutional or ideational identity at all — even roughly speaking. Art in many respects is parasitical on other social structures that fund, buy, sell and enjoy the benefits of its creations. In some measure this has always been the case. Even in ancient Greece the primary patron and benefactor of art was the political order and its rulers. Art in the Christian era has circulated more broadly and freely among different institutions and interests than in Plato's time. And, it is this relatively unencumbered circulation that attracts it to the liberal-democratic sensibility, for unlike religion art follows or promotes no official line — political, economic or religious — and remains as varied and protean as the individual artists who create it. It is the fundamental individualism of art — individual works created by individual artists — that recommends it most to any liberal-democratic ideology.[83] If the virtues of art can be found in its inherent individualism, so can its vices. The reverse side of the unencumbered circulation and protean production of art is its sheer ambiguity. What is art? What does art do? What is art for? There are many and competing aesthetic theories about the nature and purpose of art. We might be able to make some (partial) sense of these numerous theories if we return for a moment to Plato's conception of art as well as to his ideas about political order and "disorder."

---

83 It is not by accident that many modern political heroes and martyrs are not intellectuals or politicians but artists — this is especially true when one is combating political repression.

Plato's conception of art starts with the equation of truth and beauty. This overarching equivalence derives its essential meaning in the sublime identity between beauty and the good — which forms the source of all truth as represented by the sun of the Cave myth.[84] We noted that the beauty in what humans make or create — which is to say the beauty of all art broadly speaking — is mediated by the knowledge and skill of the artist. This mediation results in a work of art that can be judged beautiful when it is able to evince or represent in some fashion the truth, in other words, when it is able to find or glimpse the reality that stands behind the appearances of the empirical (which is to say, shadow) world. The connections between the good, truth and beauty and their mediation in the knowledge and skill of the artist are explicitly made and tightly drawn together by Socrates' "ideal" representation of the well-ordered *polis* in *Republic*, with the philosopher-king as the first and foremost artist of this well-ordered polity.

In conditions of disorder — which is to say in the real world of shadows — these tightly drawn connections become loosened and unraveled. As one moves from the ideal of the well-ordered city to greater and greater degrees of disorder, at least one broad distinction can be made about this movement. There are instances of disorder where the public sphere and political action (in Plato's senses of these terms) continue to function to some significant extent, while there are those instances when disorder reaches a point that the public sphere and the political activity that occurs within it become overcome and cease to exist. Whether there is a discrete and identifiable point between these two conditions of disorder is debatable, but for our purposes, unimportant. The significance of this "continuum of disorder" is that it helps us begin to understand the position art holds within liberal-democratic ideologies as a sublimation of politics and the public.

---

84   See Book VI 508 e5 and it is on the basis of this equation that meaning and intelligibility are available to human understanding at all.

If we start on the more orderly end of our continuum, we see (using Plato as our guide) that politics is the activity that works to order society in accordance with the good. Justice is the end re-sult of the political process which means, in turn, that the ordering actions of the political system are based on knowledge of things as they are rather than on their appearances (in the terminology of the Cave, they are based on knowledge of things themselves rather than knowledge of the shadows they cast). Justice, it needs to be (re)emphasized, is not equal to the good. Rather, it is informed by the good by means of an ongoing process that is continuously worked and reworked by political activity. The public sphere is the "place" where this political activity (working and re-working) oc-curs. It is not, however, a physical location. It is rather an existen-tial condition or way of life whose purposes are oriented towards knowledge of the good and to ordering society in accordance with that knowledge.

If we move further down the continuum, what happens is that "politics" becomes less concerned with truth *qua* knowledge of the good and more concerned with individual pleasures and desires, and with knowledge of the appearance of things.[85] This descent into disorder can be seen as a kind of negative "other" to the *periagoge* of the Cave, in other words, as a turning away (fully and bodily) from the good and toward the shadows. The "justice" that is realized in a substantially disordered community is, as we have argued, the natural justice of a Sophist like Thrasymachus, where justice is the interest (pleasure) of the strongest. The force of Plato's Cave myth — its elemental insight into the human condition — is perhaps best exemplified right at this point where the meanings of justice and order are highlighted against the backdrop of their negative "oth-ers." It is essential to note that the movement from order and justice towards the "other" of disorder and natural justice should not be conceived as a descent into chaos. Political disorder and the natural

85  Actually what Socrates would call opinions or beliefs (*doxa*) about things.

justice that this disorder promotes are not chaotic, *not at all*. Rather, they have an "orderliness" about them that matches if not mimics that of a well-ordered and just community. The Cave myth depicts this situation insofar as the orderliness of "things as they are" is directly matched by the orderliness of the shadows they cast. The existential problem that the myth sets up is not, therefore, one of building or restoring order out of the chaos of disorder. *The problem is instead trying to determine in what direction one is facing!*

Plato clearly believes and argues that the primary communal value of philosophy and the philosopher involves this "knowing in what direction one is facing."[86] This is moreover a function of philosophy under any and all circumstances — no matter where along the "continuum of disorder" one is located — but it becomes acute when, as in the Cave myth, a community finds itself transfixed (chained) completely in the direction of disorder, that is, pointed towards the shadows and the shadows *only*. Plato's (philosophical) assessment of his own political situation in Athens is that its citizens are predominantly pointed and fixed towards the shadows. A similar judgment can be delivered on Plato's behalf on the liberal democracies of today. Like Plato's Athens liberal-democracies are not ordered by and toward the good. They are instead ordered by and toward private human interest and pleasure. Thus, the justice that liberal democracies tend to achieve is the Thrasymachan natural justice of the strongest, which we have previously identified as its elemental Social Darwinism. It has been difficult to recognize let alone understand the true contours of Plato's assessment of his own political situation and, by implication, it is difficult for us to recognize and understand what would be his assessment of our own liberal-democratic environment. This difficulty is directly related to what I have argued is our own distorted and predominantly negative assessment of Plato's political philosophy. Our assessment

---

86   For examples of "looking both ways" types of allusions and descriptions see: Book VI 501b, Book VII 518 d5 to 519 a5, Book X 611 d5 and (as this looking relates to pleasure and happiness Book X 584 e5.-

renders the critical leverage of Plato's philosophy inoperative when it comes to evaluating liberal-democratic thought and practice. The root cause of this inoperability is an understanding of the human condition (and the structure of the world that holds it up), which fundamentally rejects Plato's myth of the Cave. This rejection means that the function and value of philosophy and the philosopher as Plato conceives them become derailed and radically reconfigured. This reconfiguration is itself directly linked to the aforementioned displacement of notions like the public sphere and political action within an all-encompassing framework that ultimately conjugates all human interests and actions into their private and economic components. To ask whether such reconfigurations and relocations that result from the ascendance of liberal-democratic ideologies are valid — in other words to ask, are they true? — is to answer the question. But this answer amounts to a return to the cave, it amounts to a return to the structure of knowledge that the Cave myth portrays. In other words it is to ask: In what direction are we facing? For Plato, the public sphere constitutes the place where this question and its answers are enacted, and politics defines those kinds of activities that occur within that "place" and whose primary purposes are to traffic in the differences between appearances and reality — in effect, to deal in matters of truth and justice. Philosophy is the discipline that informs us of these truths and the philosopher is the gadfly that (comes back down) and teaches them.

Insofar as the Cave describes something important about the elemental dynamics of the human condition, then the interest that we humans have in a public sphere — an existential place where truth is discovered and justice made — cannot simply go away (at least, not without changing something about human existence itself). Minus a public sphere and the political activity that occurs within it, our concerns with truth and justice are forced to move along and within new and different channels. One such new and major channel within the liberal-democratic complex is art.[87] Art as it is presently understood and valued fulfills in a largely subliminal manner the two functions that, in Plato's philosophy, would be more fully and openly reserved for a healthy and active public sphere. First, art links individual human beings within "communities" of shared (human) sensibilities. These communities stand in the place of our need for a robust public dimension in our life, which liberal democracies not only cannot supply, but in fact assiduously work to undermine and, where feasible, eliminate. It should be noted that these "communities" are foreshortened or truncated by the representational limits of any particular art form.[88] Second, art provides a way to look for and explore the truth and meaning of human existence. This second function is derived from the first in that it identifies artistic activity that occurs within some part of our shared humanity, while at the same time it provides a way to explore and express that humanity. When a work of art is able to evoke or portray some truth about the world and our existence within that world, it does this on the basis of our shared humanity as well as provides evidence of and insight into that humanity.

We can now see more clearly that our criticism and distaste for Plato's thoughts on his instrumental use of art (as we understand it) stem predominantly from the sublimated functions it now performs for us, both in fostering some sense of community (albeit truncated) and allowing us to look for and understand the truth in and meaning of the world and our place in it. For liberal democrats especially, *art is just too important to turn over to public officials or*

---

87   We can catch a glimpse of the future importance of art in the modern liberal democratic state in Socrates' dismissal of Homer (Book X 600 a5 -10) because his art has no public dimension or expression. This assessment is turned on its head in the modern world as the private dimension of Homer's art becomes its recommendation and the needs for public expression and truth are subliminally driven towards art ... there being, other than sectarian religions, no other place to go.

88   In this respect it is interesting to note that Wagner's concept of opera undoubtedly involved an effort to combine more and more forms of artistic expression.

*politicians.* Plato, I think, would sympathize with this reservation because he would see the fine arts in their present form and function as the one part of our existence that still makes contact with any kind of notion of truth and the good and how this might relate to human happiness within the context of human society. What I have identified as a sublimating process in art is complex in the extreme and is made only more so by the very diversity and dynamism of art in today's world. We cannot hope to put our arms around so vast and varied a subject matter within the present confines of this analysis. I wish for the moment only to reiterate and expand upon a couple points about contemporary art that I broached at the end of chapter three.

First, we noted that the value of art in the contemporary world is succumbing more and more to the (global) market forces that tend to assign and place a monetary value on anything that is or can be the object of private human interest. Of course, works of art have always been the objects of individual human desire and appreciation. In this sense art has always to some degree been coveted, bought and sold (or even simply looted by conquering armies). What is different now is that the reach, speed and sophistication of contemporary (global) market forces are becoming so pervasive and invasive that they are transforming the very content and purpose of art. The ever encroaching acquisitive market processes and the transformations that these processes put into motion are significant because there are no countervailing forces to set against them. In a (reifying) sense we can say that art is becoming completely unable to defend itself against the forces of modern global markets. Not only are liberal-democratic theory and liberal democracies unable to provide this defense on the behalf of art, they are, as we have argued, in cahoots with the predatory economic forces that are the source of the problem.

We also noted towards the end of chapter three that certain popular forms of art, like the novel and film, seem to exemplify and express the elemental and empty individualism that stands at the center of liberal-democratic thinking. The subject matter of contemporary novels and films is dominated by concerns and expositions about the individual self. This is true even when the novel or film sets out to "deconstruct" the self. No matter where one falls regarding the reality of the individual — genuine or constructed — there is no denying that it has become the major site for artistic activity by writers and filmmakers alike. Even more significant and perhaps indicative is that the appreciation and enjoyment of art, as exemplified by novels and films, has become more and more a private (sometimes even idiosyncratic) experience. Reading a book or watching a movie is an experience that is best described as solitary.[89] Moreover, the purpose of contemporary art forms is not to comment on or represent our shared humanity but to entertain us, to appeal and cater to our individual interests and desires.

It is not that the increasing privatization of art is objectionable in and of itself, even though certainly we can (and do) decry the increasing commoditization of art and bemoan its obsession with the individual, which tends to push it into idiosyncratic and disjointed directions that verge literally on the absurd. Still, these trends are a reflection of and comment on the kind of world we have made for ourselves and continue in some measure to endorse. Nor can we rightly claim that art is merely symptomatic of the conditions of our world, for surely it also helps produce and interpret that world. Rather the objection that one might make at this point — and I stress might — is that art is becoming less and less a sublimated expression of our common humanity, and thus it is becoming less able to draw us together within any kind of shared human community or experience. Indeed one of the most disturbing turns that art is beginning to take, based on the emergence and use of virtual technologies, epitomizes the trend towards privatization and away

---

89    And the movement away from the public is fairly unflagging in its consistency as we see public libraries being surmounted by Barnes and Noble stores and cinemas being replaced by home entertainment theaters.

from any kind of shared humanity and how that humanity is understood. The implications of virtual reality technologies are admittedly difficult to fully understand let alone predict, but one thing seems clear: Virtual reality happens and only happens inside the heads of individuals. If we look at this within the context of Plato's foundational myth of the Cave we can see that, with the advent of virtual reality, the cave collapses into the head of the individual (a community of one) and appearances become identical to reality.[90] (Or, if you prefer the other competing myth about the human condition, namely the Garden and the Fall of Man — with virtual reality, man becomes God.)

Well, so what? Our discussion of freedom, then equality, then truth and finally art, has consistently placed before us an existential question and, depending upon how one answers that question, an existential choice. The question is: Of what value is our common humanity, including our common understanding of it? Plato's answer is that the value of our common humanity is the realization of that humanity. Human life not lived and understood in common is in some essential measure not human at all. Liberal democrats undoubtedly would concur; after all, overtures to notions of the public good, community and justice abound in liberal-democratic discourse. But, as I have tried to demonstrate repeatedly, these overtures are echoes from a (predominantly ancient Greek) past that, even though they continue to resonate in our thoughts and practices, are unable to establish any substantial footing within them. In Plato's view, liberal-democratic theory cannot provide the conceptual nutrients and the cultivating institutional practices to make a common human life a reality. These ideological resources and the institutional practices that would build and foster a community of humans require in Plato's view that we "return to the cave." Whether we make this return or not is the existential choice we have before us and, ultimately, that is the major conclusion of

90   The popular science fiction film, *The Matrix*, deals with this kind of collapse of the world into the mind.

this book. I would like to end in the next chapter with some concluding remarks that summarize my argument and point towards what are some additional and important future areas of inquiry.

# Chapter 5. Epilogue

My analysis of Plato's political philosophy has tried to show that some of our ideas about and continued interests in justice, community and happiness are ill-served by the dominant political ideology of our time — liberal democracy. I have admittedly characterized liberal democracy in very broad strokes, even to the point of caricature. I do not claim by way of this characterization, however, that there are no significant differences among the various theories and forms of liberal democracy that fall in between the two divergent ideological endpoints I identified in chapter three as Marxist-communism and anarcho-libertarianism. I do mean to argue that there is a liberal-democratic continuum that shares certain assumptions and ideas about the human condition and the world and that these shared components deliver an interpretation of Plato that is wrongheaded and that, in its wrong-headedness, is unable to understand and nurture some of the ideas and interests that liberal democrats putatively have about such things as community, individual well-being and social justice.

I ended the last chapter with what I called an existential question. How we answer that question determines to some significant extent our estimation of the kind of world we live in and, in turn, renders a judgment about the direction we would like that world to go. I use the word "world" here in a specific sense in that, following Arendt, I am talking about the world as something that we humans make for ourselves. World can also mean more broadly speaking the cosmos or universe. This broader meaning refers to the collection of natural laws, forces and matter that provides the overarching context of the (more specifically human) "world" we make. Obviously these two worlds are related in that the world we make is largely predicated upon the kind of world that exists around us. Indeed, the existential choices we make about our human "world" are also decisions about what the structure of the larger cosmological world must be like.[91]

The existential choice as Plato sees it involves one between two opposing views of the human and natural worlds — the Socratic and the Sophistic. According to the Socratic view "the good" exists apart from humans and can be known and in some measure realized by them. The realization of the good is the source of human well-being and happiness and is, in its full measure, tied to a realization that occurs among a community of people (a city or *polis*). This communal achievement of human well-being defines a just political order. The Sophistic view conversely and flatly denies the existence of a good that exists independently of human desires and interests (man is the measure of all things). Instead, human well-being and justice are claimed to be entirely a matter of asserting and satisfying these desires and interests. The lineaments of this process are

---

91    This is in fact the relationship that is stipulated between the argument of chapter one and that of chapter two. The Cave story is Plato's rendition of what our human world looks like, and the argument of chapter two is that this human world is predicated upon a certain kind of cosmological world.

defined and determined by power. The Socratic view according to Plato is the truly human one. The Sophistic view by contrast looks upon the human condition as substantially no different from that of a pig's existence, which is Socrates' derisive way of saying that it is not substantially different than anything else in nature. I argued that liberal-democratic ideology tends to be unselfconsciously Sophistic in its outlook and that as a consequence, an elemental (albeit viral) Social Darwinism resides at its core. What complicates the picture, as we have noted on several occasions, is the advent of Christianity. It is this advent, as I indicated in chapter two, that sets the groundwork for a full- blown misinterpretation of Plato's political philosophy. By the same process, however, the Sophistic view of the world has been itself distorted by Christianity and we see the effects of this distortion in certain aspects of liberal-democratic ideology. One such aspect is how liberal-democratic thought and practice struggles with and inadvertently conceals the inherent Social Darwinism it cannot hold to its bosom but also cannot bring itself to completely disavow.

I have tried in the proceeding analysis to somewhat set the Socratic and Sophistic views back on their respective adversarial feet. Part of the reason for doing this is to gain a better understanding of Plato's political philosophy and another part is to uncover and understand some things about our own predominantly liberal-democratic ideas about politics. We can also see that the process of restoring the Socratic — Sophistic "choice" also confronts us with a question about the status or role Christianity plays within this ancient oppositional dialectic. Our discussion skirted this and other related issues so that we could begin to reestablish the original political dichotomy. Only once this is completed will we be able to take the full measure of Christianity and its relation to contemporary political thought and practice. It is my hope that the preceding analysis has gone some way towards restoring the Socratic-Sophistic dialogue. We can note at any rate that alongside what I have identified as the two existential choices that faced Plato and his fellow Athenians, a third can be added. This additional choice is predominantly a function of the emergence and establishment of Christianity, though in its current forms this additional third "choice" cannot be strictly identified with it. For simplicity's sake we can call it the transcendental choice. A more detailed characterization of this choice would hardly be simple at all. I hesitate to say much more than this for the simple reason that it would set us upon a theoretical journey as lengthy and complicated as the one we just took. Let me leave it like this: the transcendental *cum* Christian response to the existential question I posed at the end of chapter four differs from both the Socratic or Sophistic responses in three important respects. *One*, it adheres to a source of knowledge that is faith rather than reason based (admittedly, the extent and nature of this adherence is a matter of some dispute). *Two*, it posits a supernatural realm that is both the source and perfect embodiment of human well-being and justice (again the details of this "other" world are subject to dispute). *Three*, it bifurcates human existence (and only human existence in most, though not all, cases); herein humans are participants in both a natural and supernatural world. (This bifurcation is best described by the terms "body and soul"). Like the liberal-democratic complex, this "transcendental response" as I have chosen to call it comprises a wide array of ideas and practices. Further analysis of this array is required, especially in light of the distinction and differences we have (re)drawn between Plato's political philosophy and the liberal-democratic complex.

In addition to suggesting a reconsideration of the relationship of Christianity to political theory and practice, the preceding analysis sets before us three areas of further inquiry pertinent to what I have identified as Plato's "Socratic" response to matters of human well-being and justice. The first involves the mind and how it relates to the cosmos. Granted, this sounds a bit overblown (even a bit archaic or primitive) especially given our sophisticated scientific mindset.

Nevertheless some kind of accommodation or reconciliation of mind with nature (cosmos) must be met in order for Plato's philosophy to work. Plato (and the story of the Cave) presupposes an ontology that includes mind. Although our current understanding of mind is by no means settled, the scientific outlook as expressed in current cosmological theories is fairly hostile to any notion that the human mind might have an ontological status that does not conform to the naturalism of prevailing scientific theories.

The second area of inquiry concerns a revaluation of philosophy and the philosopher as a discipline and a vocation respectively. As we noted, Plato certainly draws a tight connection between politics and philosophy regardless of what condition a society and its attendant political system are in. This means that for Plato there is functionality to "doing" philosophy that has not been accurately captured by our current conceptions of it as an academic discipline and the philosopher as an academic professional.

Finally, and closely tied to the previous area of inquiry, the third area would examine what practical implications follow from Plato's political philosophy. Certainly one implication is that it provides us with a critical lever that we can use to better understand our own political landscape, and hopefully we have already been able to take advantage of that leverage in the present analysis. There are still the obvious questions about the kinds of political institutions and practices that Plato's philosophy itself recommends. I have argued that simply grafting the ideas that Plato put forth in *Republic* onto an existing political system is a dubious procedure at best; but what then is a credible one? I will conclude with a few remarks about each of these areas of inquiry.

*Mind and Cosmos.* The contemporary landscape of human knowledge is far different from the one that Plato negotiated well over two thousand years ago. One of the most significant differences in that landscape is the contemporary distinction that is currently drawn between the natural sciences and other humanistic or religious fields of inquiry. Religious fields of inquiry are related to the transcendental (mostly religious) type positions we identified in our preceding discussion about Plato's existential choice. Since these fields of inquiry are faith rather than reason based they require, as I indicated, their own separate treatment. It is moreover the distinction and difference between natural science and humanism that concerns us now, because it is a distinction that Plato would probably not have understood and most certainly would not credit. Science as its methodology is currently configured tends to dump a whole host of subjects or areas of inquiry into a hopper it identifies as "unknowable" in strictly scientific terms. The qualification that something is unknowable in scientific terms seems to present a window of opportunity for knowledge of "other" sorts to go through, and it is through this window that humanistic disciplines usually go. The subject matter of these humanistic disciplines is centered on things that deal with human interest, value, creativity and their conjoined histories. How successful or satisfying this distinction between science and humanism is remains a hotbed of discussion and disagreement. Clearly the very existence of the so-called "social" sciences indicates at least some measure of dissatisfaction with the distinction and defines efforts to bring "knowledge of humans" back into the scientific fold. The bottom line for the hard-core scientist, however, is that areas of inquiry that deal with human values, interests and creativity, including their history, are not and cannot be handled scientifically and thus cannot be known in the scientific sense — which in some quarters means that they cannot be known at all. Hard-core humanists respond for their part by ultimately denying that anything can be "known" scientifically, and thus argue in some way that even scientific knowledge is not the paragon of objectivity that scientist believe it to be. It is claimed instead that the subjectivity and humanly constructed nature of all kinds of knowledge extend and pervade into all aspects of inquiry, including any and all forms of scientific inquiry. Indeed on this view science tends to be doubly guilty because it hides behind a mislead-ing cape of objectivity. This epistemological merry-go-round has been turning in one form or another for some time now and I have no intention of taking sides or resolving it as such. Rather I will point out that Plato's position was that all systematic investiga-tion into the nature of things — human or otherwise — falls and must fall into the same epistemological bucket. Moreover, the miss-ing link in bringing all fields of knowledge — natural and human — back into the same fold is some kind of working concept mind.

What do I mean by mind? To answer that question is no doubt part of the problem. Both scientist and humanist alike identify mind, or perhaps more familiarly consciousness, as the last great frontier of human understanding. One might more accurately, di-rectly and less histrionically state that we flatly don't understand mind; we really don't get what consciousness and in particular hu-man consciousness is about or how it works. Within the interstices of our shortcomings in understanding what mind is stands the field of modern physics. Modern physics sets the ground rules for how mind must work and out of what components. As noted in chapter two this means that Plato's "three-part physics," which includes mind, energy and matter, is reduced in modern physics to two parts, namely, energy and matter. This is a reduction that leaves mind in a position of having to be derived and explained in some sense by a putatively more element combination of energy and matter.[92] This "elimination" of mind from the basic ontological set up of nature has helped set the stage both for the interpretations of Plato as a uto-pian idealist, as well as for the appeal and growth of transcendental interpretations of the human condition which resolve the problem

---

92 It can be noted that within physics itself there are the beginnings of a movement away from reductionism to what is called emergence, where mind is explained as a property that emerges from energy and matter but cannot be completely reduced (which is to say adequately explained) by its constituent material and energetic parts (see, for example Laughlin (2005). Exactly what the ontological status of an emergent property like mind is remains somewhat mysterious.

of mind/consciousness by giving it a super-natural, non-physical issue (its ontology is otherworldly).

The controversies and disagreements that exist around the topic of mind represent an open wound that has for some time (let's say since Augustine at least and not by coincidence I would add) existed in the intellectual landscape of human understanding. Philosophic disputes about topics like free will, mind and body, and the validity or reliability of knowledge itself, all point to a concept of nature that has become foreshortened in such a manner that it excludes the very thing that seems to bridge the human condition with the rest of nature. Plato's naturalism by contrast is inclusive, which means it grants the basis of human consciousness an ontological reality that is not purely derivative of the energy and matter that we now conclude make up the sum and substance of the cosmos. I concede that this represents what seems like a mere verbal formula and does not explain — specifically it does not provide the physics — that would describe and explain a cosmos that includes, on a constitutive ontological level, mind as well as energy and matter. At this juncture I conclude that a chain of reasoning (even entailment) runs from the physics we subscribe to all the way to our interests and concerns with such things as individual human wellbeing and communitarian justice. As an example of this chain I offer Plato's myth of the Cave. If this mythical image accurately captures the human condition then (a logical then), our ideas of the cosmos must in some measure support that image. If it does not — and current theories of physics do not — then one of these two complexes of ideas — Plato's myth or modern physics — must be substantially wrong. The existential bite in this "contest" as I have tried to argue in the preceding analysis is that certain cherished notions we have about human happiness and social justice are at stake.

*Philosophy and the Philosopher.* Philosophy in the modern world is first and foremost an academic profession. In this capacity it functions much in the same way as any professional activity — which is to say, that it bends to the exigencies of economic productivity and performance. Within the present analysis this means (as I noted in chapter four) that philosophy and the individuals who engage in it comprise one area of economic interest and value from among many that go about their business (literally) within the overarching liberal-democratic framework of freedom. This is not what philosophy was about in Plato's view. Part of our analysis of Plato's Cave myth tried to show that we fail to gain an understanding of Plato's ideas on philosophy and the philosopher both because we minimize the reach of the myth by making it more strictly applicable to Socrates and his situation as concerns Athenian political intrigue, and also because we tend to interpret Plato within a Christianized theoretical framework that strips his political philosophy of its existential traction and irony. Yes, the Cave myth is about Socrates, but it is also an attempt to take what Socrates represents and give it a broader theoretical expression. Socrates represents the midwife of nascent philosophers, the individual who helps achieve the *periagoge*. He is as well the gadfly on the back of a disordered (in his case Athenian) polity; he is a philosopher who "comes back down" from the mouth of the cave and the sun (the good) and testifies to the truth among and for his fellow cave dwellers. As we noted in chapter one the different movements in the Cave — the *periagoge*, the way up and the way down — are circular. This means that any philosopher, including Socrates and Plato, is engaged in any one and all of them. The roles are interchangeable and the only factor that differentiates them is time. In other words it is Socrates who "came back down" to help Plato become unchained and turned toward the light — it cannot be, in time, the other way around, though Plato in turn "comes back down" himself when he writes *Republic*.[93] It is, I have argued, Plato's intent that any philosopher at some time enacts each role of the Cave — the turn, the way up and the way back down.

---

93 The first sentence of *Republic* actually invokes the imagery of heading back down.

There are two aspects of our current understanding of philosophy that are particularly influential and tend to reinforce our standard view of Plato's philosophy. The first are our notions about the contemplative life (or what Arendt called the life of mind) and the second is our understanding of what the modern day academy represents, especially as it applies to the practice of philosophy. Our conventional ideas about what philosophy and the philosopher are about usually include some notion about the pleasures and satisfactions of contemplative thinking. It is, moreover, accurate to say that Plato is a major source of our ideas about the pleasures and satisfactions of abstract thought and even that his myth of the Cave is quite direct about making this point. The interpretive rub is whether and to what degree these avowed pleasures and satisfactions are meant to be enough or the whole story. In other words, does the contemplative life completely circumscribe what philosophy and the philosopher are about? While it is clear from Plato's Cave myth that the pleasures and satisfactions of contemplation are real and that they indeed constitute the "erotic" charge that drives the philosopher upward towards the sun *qua* the good, it is also clear that this process does not happen in a vacuum, that is, there is necessarily some kind of social-political dimension to it. This is where the second aspect comes into play, namely the academy. In our commonplace conception of things, academic life is set apart from the "real world" as a safe haven for contemplative thinking. This is true in some sense for Plato as well — but it is not the end of the story for he clearly indicates that philosophers and philosophy (academy or no) have a practical political functionality. Undoubtedly most present-day academic philosophers would not disagree. The problem is not, however, whether the academy and the scholars who work within it are a part of the greater social order or not; it is more a matter of what this relationship is and most importantly of how modern-day academic philosophers conceive of that relationship. Most appropriately, what story do philosophers tell about what it is they do? The story I contend they need to tell and ultimately abide by needs to be something very much along the lines of Plato's Cave story. Or rather, different kinds of stories will deliver very different practical conclusions. Whatever the story philosophers are telling themselves these days, a large part of that story includes philosophy as a working profession within a "working institution" of higher education. Like all of their counterparts in other "working" areas (professionals, craftsmen, laborers), they are part of an economic framework that in no small part defines and sets the terms of who they are and how they see and understand their lot in life. Once again the existential "bite" in all of this comes down to what kinds of concerns we have (if any) with matters like social justice and individual well-being. In Plato's mythical rendition of the human world there are important parts to be played by philosophy and the philosopher, parts that our predominantly liberal-democratic ide-ologies do not recognize or support.

Practically speaking, what does this mean? Assuming one is ready to agree that Plato's Cave story has purchase, that it can criti-cally illuminate our current political environment as well as suggest a different way of thinking about our common human condition — what follows? If you are a professional philosopher in a modern institution of higher learning or research for example... what is to be done? To this final question we now (very briefly) turn.

*Plato and Politics.* The relationship of theoretical philosophy to practical reality is always a matter of controversy and consterna-tion no matter what the subject matter and no matter who the thinker — and Plato is certainly no exception. Indeed his political philosophy has seemed particularly prone to this kind of controver-sy. Nearly any first-time reader of my generation can recall reading in *Republic* about the communal arrangements of the guardian class. No husbands, no wives, no sons or daughters...no family! — *Is this Plato mad?* And, as we have seen in the analysis above there is more — there is plenty.

Part of the problem, as I have argued, stems from a quick and ready inclination among both first-time and even seasoned readers alike to take Plato (via Socrates) at his word, to simply conclude that, all things being equal, the basic form and substance of *Republic* are what humans should strive to implement in their own political environment. Of course not only are "all things" not equal, they are as I have tried to argue not even the same! The difference is the world that we live in is, for better or worse, a world that is predominantly a world of shadows. And it is because of the immediacy and permanence of this shadow world that the truth and stability of ideas (the "reality" that stands behind the shadows) can never be fully expressed or instantiated in it. To completely get at the reality behind the shadows would require, as I argued in chapter two, that the cave collapse unto itself, that appearances and reality become one and the same. At no point that I am aware of does Plato remotely suggest that this can happen (and it is why Socrates identifies the truly just polity of *Republic* as more a dream than a reality).

It can be noted at this juncture, and as part of the reexamination of Christianity and politics that I suggest and recommend above, that the "incarnation" of the Word in the body of Christ is precisely a collapsing of the cave, and it is most certainly because of this collapse — as well as its near universal (western) appeal and acceptance — that we are led to interpretations of Plato's political philosophy that are fundamentally off the mark. I maintain that Plato's argument is that in order for human thought and action to work, a "safe and unbridgeable distance" must be drawn and patrolled between appearances and reality. Only then can a productive and accurate arrangement be established and managed between appearances and reality. It is the idea of the philosopher-king that paradoxically yet quite emphatically makes this point.

There is nothing about the idea of the philosopher-king or the just polity that cultivates and nurtures him and which he in turn rules that is, strictly speaking, impossible. Socrates in fact is at pains to make this point. At the same time he is also keen to point out that the philosopher-king constitutes an extremely high order of improbability, a kind of perfect alignment of the stars. It is important to note however that this improbability points in two directions. One direction is genetic — how are the conditions of truth and justice (and the philosopher-king) to be generated? This is what Socrates talks about in the first part of *Republic*. The other direction is historical — how can truth and justice once realized (in some sense in and by virtue of the very existence of a philosopher-king) be maintained, or to use Socrates' formulation, what happens to the just polity (and its philosopher-king ruler) when it is put in motion? This is what Socrates talks about in the second part of *Republic*. It is hardly accidental that these two parts are separated by the myth of the Cave. The generation and maintenance of a political order that aspires to be just (the patrolling and working on what I have called the "distance" between appearance and reality) are represented by the movements within the cave — turn from, up towards and back down from — which as I have argued are circular (occurring all the time) and interchangeable (occurring in the same person over time). What the idea of the philosopher-king represents, albeit paradoxically, is the need to keep the circle circular. Otherwise, philosophers go one way and kings, another — meaning that knowledge and politics part company (unfortunately an all too accurate portrayal of contemporary liberal-democratic politics). The first immediate lesson that Plato's political philosophy teaches us is to work to keep knowledge and politics together while patrolling and maintaining the distance and difference between appearances and the reality that stands behind them — a distance and difference which Sophists and Christians alike regularly deny and disregard — I would add, at their own risk.

***

I am not sanguine enough to believe that, by virtue of the words I have written here, somehow a constructive dialogue and inter-action will begin between philosophy and politics. Quite frankly neither may be ready for the other. At the same time I must testify to what I believe is true about the world we live in, the things we cherish and the kinds of people we aspire to become. If nothing else it is a beginning — a turn, a way up and...a way back down.

# BIBLIOGRAPHY

Arendt, Hannah. *The Human Condition*. The University of Chicago Press , 1958.

Bernardete, Seth (translator). *Plato's Symposium* (with Commentary by Allan Bloom) University of Chicago Press, 1993.

Brinton, Crane. *Ideas & Men: The Story of Western Thought*. Prentice-Hall, 1962.

Habermas, Jurgen. *Legitimation Crisis*, (translated by Thomas McCarthy). Beacon Press, 1975.

Kimlicka, Will. *Liberalism, Community and Culture*. Clarendon Press, 1989.

Laughlin, Robert. *A Different Universe*. Basic Books, 2005.

MacIntyre, Alasdair. *A Short History of Ethics*. MacMillan, 1966.

Popper, Karl. *The Open Society and its Enemies*. Harper & Row, 1962.

Rawls, John. *A Theory of Justice*. Belknap Press, 1971.

Sabine, George & Thorson, Thomas. *A History of Political Theory*. Dryen Press, 1973.

Sandel, Micheal. *Democracy's Discontents*. Belknap Press, 1996.

Taylor, Charles. *Sources of Self: The Making of the Modern Identity*. Harvard University Press. 1992.

Voeglin, Eric. *Plato*. Louisiana State University Press, 1966.

Wiser, James. *Political Philosophy: A History of the Search for Order*. Prentice-Hall, 1983

Wolin, Sheldon. *Politics and Vision*. Little, Brown & Company, 1960.

# INDEX